THE FOOTFALL'S ECHO

An Anthology from Norfolk's Past

THE FOOTFALL'S ECHO

An Anthology from Norfolk's Past

Edited by
NICHOLAS SIMMS

Drawings by Colin Bygrave

ORLANDO PUBLISHING
Chequers Cottage
Church Lane
Briston
Norfolk NR24 2LF

First published in 1989 by
Orlando Publishing
Briston Norfolk
Printed by Witley Press Ltd
Hunstanton Norfolk
© 1989 by Nicholas Simms
ISBN 1 870982 04 5

Contents

	page
Preface	7
Foreword	8
Introduction	9
Origins	13
Everyday Life	19
Farmers, Fish and Wool	37
Mainly Illegal	59
Some Memorable People	71
The View from Outside	79

Time present and time past
Are both perhaps present in time future,
And time future contained in time past.
If all time is eternally present
All time is unredeemable.
What might have been is an abstraction
Remaining a perpetual possibility
Only in a world of speculation.
What might have been and what has been
Point to one end, which is always present.
Footfalls echo in the memory
Down the passage which we did not take
Towards the door we never opened
Into the rose-garden. My words echo
Thus, in your mind.
                    But to what purpose
Disturbing the dust on a bowl of rose-leaves
I do not know.
                    Other echoes
Inhabit the garden. Shall we follow?

T.S. Eliot
Four Quartets

Preface

Alfred the Great, in his preface to an anthology drawn from St Augustine's 'Soliloquies', used a metaphor which is as fresh and apt today as it was in the late 9th Century. A man gathers wood in a forest, a store of wood which is open to all to make use of. No better description of, or justification for, anthologies has ever been written.

Then I gathered for myself staves and props and bars and handles for all the tools I knew how to use, and cross bars and beams for all the structures which I knew how to build, the fairest pieces of timber, as many as I could carry. I neither came home with a single load, nor did it suit me to bring home all the wood, even if I could have carried it. In each tree I saw something that I required at home. For I advise each of those who is strong and has many wagons, to plan to go to the same wood where I cut these props, and fetch for himself more there, and load his wagons with fair rods, so that he can plait many a fair wall, and put up many a peerless building, and build a fair enclosure with them; and may dwell therein pleasantly and at his ease winter and summer, as I have not yet done . . .

Foreword

The sources from which this book is drawn run from the 1st century A.D. to 1976. Passages from before 1400 have been translated into modern English. A few, very minor, changes have been made to extracts from the 15th century to make them fully comprehensible to the modern reader. All later passages appear as they were originally printed.

Most of the contributors need no special introduction, but as The Paston Letters and James Woodforde's Diary inevitably make several appearances, a few words should be said about each.

The Paston family came from the Norfolk village of that name and rose during the 15th century to become one of the most prominent families in East Anglia. They espoused the royalist cause during the Civil War and, in consequence, were heavily penalised. Although ennoblement came after the Restoration, the family's finances never recovered and the line died with the second Earl of Yarmouth in 1732, whose estates had to be sold to pay his debts. The Paston Letters are a collection of letters and documents written in the 15th and early 16th centuries. They cover every aspect of life: love affairs, business, war and, as many of the Pastons served as Members of Parliament, politics. There is no other collection of papers that gives us such a comprehensive picture of late medieval life.

James Woodforde was born in Somerset in 1740 and followed his father into Holy orders. He was presented to the living of Weston Longueville, in Norfolk, in 1774, but did not take up residence there until 1776. He died in the Parsonage on January 1, 1803. His diary runs from 1758 until the autumn of 1802, a period that takes in the American and French Revolutions, the first half of the Napoleonic wars and the beginning of the Industrial Revolution, but you would only have to skip a few of his entries to miss these great events entirely. His life was uneventful, his interests unremarkable, yet his Diary is wholly absorbing because he had a novelist's eye for the significant detail which can transform a commonplace event into a unique moment. His simple catalogue of a comfortable rural life enables us, as his near-contemporary William Blake put it, 'To see the World in a Grain of Sand, and a Heaven in a Wild Flower.'

Introduction

In his prologue to *The Go-Between*, L.P. Hartley wrote, in a sentence that is already passing into cliche, *'The past is a foreign country: they do things differently there'*. It is a fine piece of aphoristic writing: simply phrased yet profound. Like most aphorisms, however, it expresses only a partial truth. People in the past did many of the same things we do for the same reasons, they did the same things for different reasons, and they did different things altogether, for reasons we can barely comprehend. We can, for instance, understand that, for the medieval well-to-do, marriage was a matter of financial convenience and had little to do with love, but we cannot really enter the mind of a 16th century witch-hunter, for we no longer live in a world where the supernatural is an ever-present reality and sorcery a likely cause of many of our woes. We cannot unlearn the discoveries of science and the facts of evolution; nor can we now live in a world of faith without denying our faculty of reason. The developed countries have changed more in the last 150 years than in the previous 1,000, and people's mental outlook has changed at the same time. Of course there was change and development in the pre-industrial world, but it was very slow by today's standards. The 18th century farm labourer theoretically had more freedom than a medieval villein, but his life had changed very little: its main elements were still drudgery and poverty. (In many ways the villein could be said to have been better off: he probably had a few strips of land in the open fields round his village and access to common land for his livestock). Both would have more in common with each other than either would have with a modern office or factory worker. It may be a truism to say that we live in a new, different world, but it is of the essence of truisms that they do express a truth. For over 5,000 years, from the introduction of farming until the Industrial Revolution, at least 90% of Britain's inhabitants were country dwellers; by 1830 half the population lived in towns or cities: now over 90% do so. Even in a county as rural as Norfolk, less than 4% of the workforce is directly involved in agriculture.

Small though the agricultural sector now seems, it is, and has always been, of immense importance. Civilisation grew on its back. In the early Middle Ages the yield ratio for grain crops was about 1:3. That means that for every grain planted at sowing time only 3 were harvested and, of course, one of those grains had to be stored for next year's seed. At that level of production there is an insufficient surplus available to feed more than a very small number of non-agricultural workers. It is said that a yield ratio of 1:5 is necessary before significant industry or commerce can develop. That level was reached by the 14th century. Yields have continued to rise: 1:7 was normal in the 17th century, 1:10 in the nineteenth and 1:15 in the middle of this century. By using modern fertilisers, farmers now routinely achieve a yield ratio of 1:30. 'Civilised' society may dwarf the farming industry, but it is still utterly dependent on it. Cars and computers are useful but they do not make good eating. In our highly-mechanised modern world, farming gives us a direct link to the Neolithic Revolution of about 3,000 B.C. THE revolution that enabled man to begin to manage his environment rather than compete with the wolves and the birds for wild foods. (Whether it was a good thing or a bad thing for man to learn to manage, or mismanage, the natural world is a different, sombre question).

Although material conditions and mental attitudes have been transformed, much of everyday human behaviour remains the same. Birth, copulation, death and the necessity to eat are the fixed essentials of human existence. There are many passages in this book that will induce a thrill of recognition in the reader, although there are two interconnected areas of human behaviour that *have* changed substantially. Women are now regarded — save by certain religious demoninations — as fully (well, almost) paid-up members of the human race. On the other hand children, once considered blessings or assets, are more often thought of as liabilities: in consequence our fertility rate has dropped to an historically very low level, lower probably than in pre-Neolithic hunter-gatherer days.

That comparison may seem strange, but only because humans suffer from what one might call 'temporal provincialism'. We find it very hard to think in long time-scales. We may know intellectually that we are closer in time to William the Conqueror than he was to Julius Caesar, but we don't fully comprehend it. They both belong to too distant a past for our brains, evolved to cope with a single lifetime, to place in a time-scale that we can visualise. The dying heavy industries of the North and our trading links with what is now called the Commonwealth, are both often referred to as 'traditional' when, in fact, they only flourished for about 150 years, a fairly short period in our history. We were exporting wool, cloth and fish to Europe for over 500 years before Australia was even discovered. (Always beware when someone appeals to tradition: they are trying to sell you something, whether it be overpriced, 'traditional' mustard or a political idea based on a very selective view of the past, or they are attempting to justify their entrenched privileges. Churchill, a rare politician with a sense of history, had few illusions about the past. 'Don't talk to me about naval tradition', he once said. 'It's nothing but rum, sodomy and the lash.') This is not to say that the past has no value to us today: quite the opposite in fact. We can learn much from history. Our most valuable tradition, and the most frequently endangered, developed in the Middle Ages: the concept that people and corporations have rights that the state cannot infringe.

What, you might well ask, has all this got to do with an anthology from Norfolk's past? It's a question of historical perspective. In almost any rural area, if one has any imagination at all, the past is a constant presence. Our landscape is littered with Neolithic barrows, Iron Age forts, medieval churches, deserted villages and coastal ports shorn of their trade by the coming of the railways, to remind us that we are very short-term tenants in time and space. Things that seem of importance to us today, may well not seem so in a hundred years. Will a car factory have a useful life comparable to that of an 18th century barn, let alone a Norman church? Whatever the future brings (assuming that we don't destroy ourselves by polluting the planet) there will be farmers — and, of course, lawyers to sort out, for a fee, disputes between neighbours.

Origins

The Iceni Rebel

The rebellion of Boudicca (or Boadicea) in A.D. 61 is one of the most famous episodes in British history. The Iceni of East Anglia, whose heartlands seem to have been in the Norwich area and in North West Norfolk, were left unmolested by the Romans after their King, Prasutagus, offered his submission. On his death he made the Emperor Nero co-heir to his small kingdom with his two daughters, in the hope that his people's relative independence would continue. The Roman historian Tacitus tells us what actually transpired ...

Kingdom and household were plundered like prizes of war, the one by Roman officers, the other by Roman slaves. As a beginning, his widow Boudicca was flogged and their daughters raped. The Icenian chiefs were deprived of their hereditary estates as if the Romans had been given the whole country. The King's own relatives were treated like slaves.

No wonder they rebelled! They burnt and slaughtered in Colchester, St Albans and London. 'The British did not take or sell prisoners', *wrote Tacitus.* 'They could not wait to cut throats, hang, burn, and crucify...' *In London, according to another classical historian, Dio Cassius...*

They hung up naked the noblest and most distinguished women and then cut off their breasts and sewed them to their mouths, in order to make the victims appear to be eating them; afterwards they impaled the women on sharp skewers run lengthwise through the body. All this they did to the accompaniment of sacrifices, banquets and wanton behaviour, not only in all their other sacred places, but particularly in the grove of Andate.

The savage leader of this vengeful mob was described by Dio ... She was very tall, in appearance terrifying, in the glance of her eye most fierce, and her voice was harsh; a great mass of the tawniest hair fell to her hips; around her neck she wore a large golden necklace; and she wore a tunic of divers colours over which a thick mantle was fastened with a brooch. This was her invariable attire.

She did not have a high regard for the Romans, if her reported speeches are to be believed ... 'Don't fear the Romans! ... They protect themselves with helmets, breastplates and greaves ... They can't stand hunger, thirst, cold or heat, as we can. They need shade and covering, kneaded bread and wine and oil ... (they are) men who bathe in warm water, eat artificial dainties, drink unmixed wine, anoint themselves with myrrh, sleep on soft couches with boys for bedfellows — boys past their prime at that — and are slaves to a lyre-player and a poor one too.'

Despite her contempt, Suetonius Paulinus defeated the Iceni and Boudicca is said to have poisoned herself. The Romans claimed to have killed almost 80,000 Britons for the loss of only 400 legionaries. Whatever the real British losses, the battle was clearly a decisive victory for the invaders. It has been plausibly suggested that the Roman road now known as the Peddars Way was built soon after the revolt to give the legions quick access to the tribal lands of the Iceni when necessary.

An Antiquarian's Speculations

If a map of Norfolk had survived from the tenth century A.D. it would be instantly recognisable today, for almost all our modern place names would appear, albeit differently spelt. The great majority are Anglo-Saxon names: those ending in -ham, -ing, -ingham, -ton, -wich, -ford, and -field are the most common. After the establishment of the Danelaw in the 9th century Norse endings such as -by and -thorpe appeared. Apart from a few names revealing Roman origins, like Brancaster, Caister and Eccles, most of our evidence of earlier settlements comes from archaeology. In 1658, when Sir Thomas Browne wrote Urne Buriall, the science was in its infancy and he was wrong in ascribing an Anglo-Saxon cemetery to the Romans ...

In a field of old *Walsingham*, not many moneths past, were digged up between fourty and fifty Urnes, deposited in a dry and sandy soil, not a yard deep, nor farre from one another: Not all strictly of one figure, but most answering these described: some containing two pounds of bones, distinguishable in skulls, ribs, jawes, thigh-bones and teeth, with fresh impressions of their combustion. Besides the extraneous substances, like peeces of small boxes, or combes handsomely wrought, handles of small brasse instruments, brazen nippers, and in one some kinde of Opale.

That these were the urnes of *Romanes* from the common custome and place where they were found, is no obscure conjecture, not farre from a *Romane Garrison*, and but five Miles from *Brancaster*, set down by ancient Record under the name of *Brannodunum*.

But his speculations about the origin of Norwich were correct, although we now know that the site of Venta Icenorum was what is now Caistor St Edmund.

... the City of Norwich arose from the ruins of *Venta*, and though perhaps not without some habitation before, was enlarged, builded, and nominated by the *Saxons*. In what bulk or populosity it stood in the old East-Angle Monarchy tradition and history are silent. Considerable it was in the *Danish* eruptions, when *Sueno* burnt *Thetford* and *Norwich*, and *Ulfketel*, the Governor thereof, was able to make some resistance, and after endeavoured to burn the *Danish* navy.

Viking Vengeance

The Anglo-Saxon Chronicle reports that in 1002 Ethelred Unraed (no counsel) ordered a massacre of the Danes living in England. No doubt this was effective in Wessex, but could not have been carried out in areas of the Danelaw like Norfolk, which had had a substantial, dominant Scandinavian population for over 100 years. Nevertheless, Svein Forkbeard, King of Denmark, was able to combine the motives of the blood-feud and financial gain when he attacked in 1003-1005. In 1003 he concentrated on Wessex and 'took much booty'. In 1004 he arrived in Norfolk.

Svein came with his fleet to Norwich, ravaged all the borough and burnt it down. Then Ulfcytel advised, with the counsellors of East Anglia, that it would be better for them to buy peace from the force before they did too much harm in the land, because they had come without warning, and he did not have time to gather his troops. Under the truce which should have been between them, the force stole up from the ships and went their way to Thetford. When Ulfcytel saw that, he sent word that the ships should be hewn apart, but those he had in mind for this failed; then he gathered his troops secretly as quickly as he could. The force came to Thetford within three weeks of ravaging Norwich, and were there for one night, ravaged the borough and burnt it down. In the morning they meant to go to their ships, and Ulfcytel came with his host, they came resolutely together, and many dead fell

on either hand. The most senior of the East Anglian people were killed, but if their full strength had been there, they would never have been
able to get back to their ships; they themselves said that they had never
met with harder hand-play in England than Ulfcytel gave them.

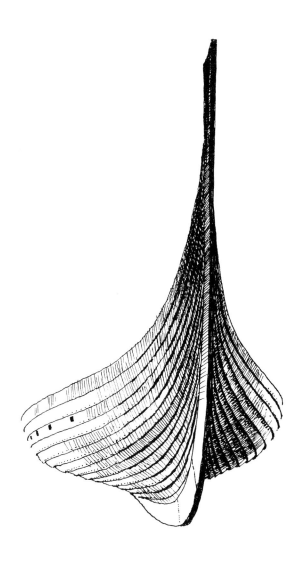

In 1010 the Danes were back in East Anglia and defeated their old enemy Ulfcytel Snilling at Ringmere near Thetford, after the cowardly defection of Thurcytel.

The force, (*having wintered in Kent*), came after Easter to East Anglia, landed at Ipswich, and went straight on to where they had heard that Ulfcytel was with his troops; this was on the first day of Ascension. The East Anglians soon fled; Cambridgeshire stood firmly against them. There was killed Aethelstan, the king's son in law, Oswi, his son, Eadwig, Aefic's brother, Wulfric, Leofwine's son, and many other good thanes, countless folk; the flight was first started by Thurcytel Mare's Head, and then the Danes had the power of the battlefield. There they were horsed, and after had control of East Anglia. For three months in that land they ravaged and burnt, killed men and cattle, and burnt throughout the fens. They burnt down Thetford and Cambridge, and afterwards went southward into the Thames valley.

The First Census

The popular image of the early Middle Ages is of a few hovels scattered in clearings in the midst of impenetrable forest. This was not so, especially in Norfolk which, even in 1086 when the Domesday Book was compiled, had a population of about 100,000. Norwich and Thetford had both recovered from the depredations of the Vikings and each had some 5,000 inhabitants. About 500 people lived in Yarmouth, of whom 24 were fishermen. The rest of the more than 700 places named and described were agricultural villages. Some have grown since . . .

King Edward held DISS before 1066, 480 acres of land as a manor.
14 villeins; 24 smallholders; 2 slaves.
1 plough in lordship; 18 men's ploughs.
Meadow, 10 acres. A church, 24 acres.
7 head of cattle, 11 sheep, 5 goats.

Some estates had already got beyond subsistence farming and were obviously producing wool on a commercial scale . . .

St Benedict the Benedictine monastery at Ramsey, Hunts has always held BRANCASTER.
3 ploughs in lordship; 7 men's ploughs.

25 villeins, 16 smallholders; 5 slaves.
Meadow, 2 acres; 1 mill.
5 smallholders, 6 acres.
Also 60 acres of land which have always been in lordship.
2 cobs; 6 head of cattle; 24 pigs; 600 sheep.
The whole has one league in length and ½ in width, tax of 28d.

Some shrank ...

(Castle) RISING, 360 acres.
12 villeins; 38 smallholders; 3 slaves.
Meadow, 14 acres. Always 2 ploughs in lordship, 2 men's ploughs.
Also 7 Freemen, 24 acres of land.
1 plough, 3 mills; 12 salt-houses; 1 fishery.
Also 3 Freemen, 60 acres of land; 1 plough.
Also 1 Freeman, 60 acres; 1 plough.
24 smallholders.
1 plough; meadow, 8 acres; 1 mill; 1 salt-house.

*Note. The figures given for inhabitants are for heads of household. The
total population would have been 3 to 4 times greater, giving Castle Rising
a total of around 300.*

Everyday Life

A Cheery Parson

The Black Death of 1348-50 killed about a third of the population of Europe. Norwich suffered particularly badly: probably half of its inhabitants died and it did not regain its lost citizens until the end of the sixteenth century. The long term effects were profound, especially on men's minds. The Church taught that God had sent the catastrophe as a punishment for the sins of man. It is at this period that the grisly skeletons appear in church and churchyard saying 'As I am, so shall you be'. Here, from the Paston papers, is an extract from the sort of cheerful sermon you might have heard delivered had you lived in the fifteenth century. Its overall theme is that you cannot enjoy this world if your behaviour puts you in fear of divine retribution in the next: the only real joy on earth is the joy of contemplating the eternal bliss to come.

'Friends, you owe for to ask of God that your joy may be a full joy and perfect. We may never have a full joy in this world, where as ever among follows grief. A man delights sometimes in gold and silver and in great substance of earthly goods, in the beauty of women; but this joy is not perfect, is not stable, but is as mutable as a shadow, for it may happen that he that rejoices in the beauty of his wife may follow her to church on a bier tomorrow ...

There be three manner of joys, the one empty, another half full, the third is full joy. The first is plenty of worldly goods, the second is spiritual grace, the third is everlasting bliss. The first joy, that is affluence of temporal goods, is called a vain joy, for if a man were set at a board with delicate meats and drinks, and he saw a cauldron boiling before him with pitch and brimstone in the which he should be thrown naked as soon as he had dined, though he should joy much in his delicious meats it would be a vain joy. Thus is the joy of a covetous man; if he could see what pain his soul would suffer in hell for his miskeeping and getting of his goods he should not joy in his treasure.'
(James Gloys c.1470)

Earthly Joys

Despite James Gloys, churchmen and their wives are fallible human be-
ings, like us. John Aubrey's Brief Lives contains the following entry con-
cerning John Overall (1560-1618). He ended as Bishop of Norwich after
a long and distinguished career in the Church, including a spell as Dean
of St Pauls. He was obviously a tolerant man, for his wife appears to have
had an exceptionally warm nature..

I Know not what he wrote or whether he was any more than a
common-prayer Doctor: but most remarqueable by his Wife, who was
the greatest Beautie of her time in England. That she was so, I have it
attested from the famous Limmer Mr. Hoskins, and other old Painters,
besides old Courtiers. She was not more beautiful than she was obligeing
and kind, and was so tender-hearted that (truly) she could scarce denie
any one. She had (they told me) the loveliest Eies that were ever seen,
but wondrous wanton.When she came to Court, or to the Play-house, the
Gallants would so flock about her. Richard, the Earle of Dorset, and his
brother Edward, since Earle, both did mightily adore her. And by their
report he must have had a hard heart that did not admire her ...

The good old Deane, notwithstanding he knew well enough he was
horned, loved her infinitely: in so much that he was willing she should
enjoy what she had a mind to.
Among others who were charmed by her was John Selby, of
Yorkshire. Old Mris. Tyndale (who knew her) remembers a song made
of her and Sir John, part whereof was this, viz:
> The Deane of St Paule's did search for his wife,
> and where d'ee thinke he found her?
> Even upon Sir John Selbye's bed,
> as flatte as any Flounder.

Richard Corbett (1582-1635) was another bishop of Norwich who
featured in Brief Lives. Aubrey's slanderous suggestion that his marriage
was incestuous is almost certainly untrue.

His Chaplain, Dr. Lushington, was a very learned and ingeniose
man, and they loved one another. The Bishop sometimes would take
the key of the wine-cellar, and he and his Chaplaine would goe and
lock themselves in and be merry. Then first he layes downe his
Episcopall hat — *There lyes the Doctor.* Then he puts off his gowne

— There lyes the Bishop. Then twas, *Here's to thee Corbet,* and *Here's to thee, Lushington.*

He married Alice Hutton, whom 'twas sayd he bigott. She was a very beautifull woman, and so was her mother.

Staff Difficulties

If the clergy did not always maintain the highest standards of sexual morality, it is scarcely surprising that the laity have always indulged in what Mark Twain called 'the one ecstasy that stands first and foremost in the heart of every individual'. But when the servants do it, it upsets the tenor of the household. In 1472 Edmund Paston was quite prepared to forget his excellent servant's peccadilloes, but his mother was not.

Sire, I recommend me to you. Please it you to weet that my mother hath caused me to put Gregory out of my service; as God help, I write to you the very cause why. It happened him to have a knaves lust, in plain terms to swive a prostitute; and so did in the rabbit warren. It fortuned him to be espied by two ploughmen of my mother's, which were as fain as he of that matter, and desired them to have part; and as fellowship required, said not nay, in so much that the ploughmen had her all night in their stable and Gregory was clean delivered of her and, as he swears, had nothing to do with her in my mother's place. Not withstanding my mother thinks that he was the ground of that matter, wherefore there is no remedy but he must leave . . .

A friend of Parson Woodforde's also had servant problems.

1789 March 4, Wednesday

. . . Mr Du Quesne dined and spent the Aft. with us. He was not in good Spirits, owing to disagreeable things happening in his Family with regard to Servants, his Man Servant James Atterton having been too familiar with his two young Servant Maids, Lizzy Greaves, an old Servant Maid of Mine about 23 Years of Age, and another Girl by name Mary, both of which are with Child by James. The former Maid Lizzy, was married Yesterday to James, and the other discovered her Situation only last Night. James also had kept Company with Lizzy's Sister, Sukey, now Servant at Weston House for the last four Years. James never appeared to have been such a sly Fellow as he has proved to be, but much the contrary . . .

Marriage

If relations between the sexes have always been much the same, no doubt the small change of married life has varied little. Children's clothes and naughty goings-on up the road must ever have been subjects of conversation. Margaret Paston writes to her husband in 1444 ...

'I pray you that ye will vouchsafe to buy for me such lace as I send you example of in this letter, and one piece of black lace. As for caps that ye sent me for the children, they be too little for them. I pray you buy them finer caps and larger than those were ... Heydon's wife had child on St. Peter's Day. I heard tell that her husband will nought of her, nor of her child that she had last neither. I heard tell that he said if she come in his presence to make her excuse that he should cut off her nose to make her be known what she is, and if her child come in his presence he said he would killen. He will not be entreated to have her again in no wise, as I heard tell.

The Bastardy Act of 1733 resulted in many forced marriages. Under it a man had to marry the woman he had impregnated, or indemnify the parish against future Poor Law costs, on pain of imprisonment. As most men were poor they had no choice but to marry.

Jan 25th 1787
... Rode to Ringland this Morning and married one Robert Astick and Elizabeth Howlett by Licence, Mr Carter being from home, and the Man being in Custody, the Woman being with Child by him. The Man was a long time before he could be prevailed on to marry her when in the Church Yard; and at the Altar behaved very unbecoming. It is a cruel thing that any Person should be compelled by Law to marry. I recd. of the Officers for marrying them 0. 10. 6. It is very disagreeable to me to marry such Persons ...
(Woodforde)

A Realist

Trollope hated 'those words 'an excellent marriage'. In them is contained more of wicked worldliness than any other words one ever hears spoken.' *Although nowadays we generally marry for reasons of sexual attraction, mothers still tell their daughters that it is as easy to fall in love with a rich man as a poor man. In the past they were quite straight forward about it . Here Edmond Paston, in 1480, writes of a potential wife in terms that sound more suited to the second hand car trade than to romance: low mileage, only one owner, a wealth of accessories . . .*

Here is lately fallen a widow in Worstead which was wife to one Bolt, a worsted merchant, and worth £1,000, and gave to his wife one hundred marks in money, household goods and plate to the value of 100 marks, and ten pounds per year in land. She is called a fair gentlewoman . . . and has but 2 children which shall be at the dead's charge. She was his wife but 5 years.

A Romantic

In the late 1690s The Rev. William Nevar wrote to his former pupil, Ashe Windham, of Felbrigg Hall.

Sir,

I date this letter from the happiest day of my life, a Levitical Conjurer transformed me this morning from an Insipid, Unrelishing Batchelour into a Loving Passionate Husband, but in the midst of all the raptures of approaching Joys, some of my thoughts must fly to Felbrigg, and tho I am called away 17 times in a minute to new exquisite dainties, yet I cannot resist the inticing temptation of conversing with you, and acquainting you, with tears in my Eyes, that I am going to lose my Maidenhead, but you'll think perhaps of the old Saying, that some for Joy do cry, and some for Sorrow sing. Colonel Finch, who honours us with his merry company, tells me of the dismall dangers I am to run before the next Sun shines upon me, but the Spouse of my bosom being of a meek, forgiving temper, I hope she will be mercifull, and not suffer a young beginner to dye in the Experiment. I commend myself to your best prayers in this dreadfull Juncture, and wishing you speedily such a happy night, as I have now in prospect.

I remain
Your most humble and
most obedient Servant
W. Nevar

A Woman's Place

Lady Catherine Sarah Elliot, third daughter of the Earl of Minto, was married to Sir John Boileau of Ketteringham Hall. She died in 1862, after a life that most modern women would not consider fulfilled, although she had the normal Victorian complement of nine children. In 1835 she wrote out a series of questions to ask herself each evening. She sets an admirable example for her sex, although, I must admit, my wife does not agree with my judgement ...

Have I been dutiful and affectionate in my manner, as well as in my feelings, towards my dear husband this day?

Have I listened to him when speaking to me, with *attention*, with a desire to understand his meaning, with a readiness to enter into his views, to agree with his opinions?

Have I guarded against my disposition to contradict and to find objections to what he says?

Have I taken care neither to be sulkily silent, or hasty in answering him, in conversation?

Have I submitted with a *cheerful humility* when he has thought right to reprove me for or point out any of my faults?

Have I resisted with all my strength all desire to *defend* myself even if I should have not seen my fault?

Have I felt grateful for his advice and admonition, and *tried sincerely* to believe his motive is to do me good?

Have I shewn myself ready to arrange my occupations to suit his hours and his convenience, and that without tormenting him with questions?

Have I tried in *everything* to consult his wishes?

Have I prayed earnestly for the assistance of God for my Saviour's sake, in all these duties *not relying* too much on my *own strength*?

A Feckless Son

In 1465 John Paston wrote to his wife about his eldest son. Many of his complaints have a modern ring, but the assumption that children are produced to help and profit their parents, though common in undeveloped countries, is no longer general in the West.

'Item, as for your son: I let you weet I would he did well, but I understand in him no disposition of policy nor of governance as a man of the world ought to do, but only liveth, and ever hath, as man dissolute, without any provision; nor that he busieth himself nothing to understand such matters as a man of livelihood must needs understand. Nor I understand nothing of what disposition he purposeth to be, but only I can think he would dwell again in your house and mine, and there eat and drink and sleep. Therefore I let you weet I would know him ere he know mine intent, and how well he hath occupied his time now he hath had leisure. Every poor man that hath brought up his childer to the age of 12 years waiteth* then to be helped and profited by his childer, and every gentleman that hath discretion waiteth* that his kin and servants that liveth by him and at his cost should help him forward. As for your son, ye know well he never stood you nor me in profit, ease, or help to value of one groat, saving at Caldecott Hall, when he and his brothers kept it one day against Debenham ...'

A Grateful Daughter

We are often told that parents were much stricter with their children in the past. Although it was certainly true of those deeply unappealing people, the Victorian middle classes, it beggars belief that it has always and generally been so. The Norfolk rector, Michael Browne, was obviously an indulgent father, as his daughter Charlotte Elizabeth's Personal Reminiscences (1841) show.

'Often would my father take his noble pointers, preparatory to the shooting season, at once to try their powers and to ascertain what promise of future sport the fields presented. These were destructive expeditions in one sense. I remember the following dialogue, repeated to me by my brother, when we made our appearance at home after a day's demolition of wearing apparel.

*wait is used here in the obsolete meaning of expect.

26

"Mr B. this will never do; that girl cannot wear a frock twice without soiling it; nor keep it whole for a week: the expense will ruin us."

"Well my dear, if I am to be ruined by expense, let it come in the shape of the washerwoman's and linen-draper's bills; not in those of the apothecary and undertaker."

My dear father was right; and it would be a happy thing for girls in general if somewhat of appearance, and of acquirement too, was sacrificed to what God has so liberally provided, and to the enjoyment of which a blessing is undoubtedly annexed . . . It positively pains me to see a party of girls, bonneted and tippeted double file of humanity, 'That like a wounded snake drags its slow length along' under the keen surveillance of a governess, whose nerves would never be able to endure the shock of seeing them bound over a stream or scramble through a fence, or even toss their heads and throw out their limbs as all young animals, except that oppressed class called young ladies, are privileged to do. Having ventured, in a fit of country daring, to break the ice of this very rigid and frigid subject, I will recount another instance of the paternal good sense to which I owe, under God, the physical powers without which my little talent might have lain by a napkin all my days.

One morning, when his daughter was about eight years old, my father came in, and found sundry preparations going on, the chief materials for which were buckram, whalebone, and other stiff articles; while the young lady was under measurement by the hands of a female friend.

"Pray what are you going to do to the child?"

"Going to fit her with a pair of stays."

"For what purpose?"

"To improve her figure; no young lady can grow up properly without them."

"I beg your pardon; young gentlemen grow up very well without them and so may young ladies."

"Oh, you are mistaken. See what a stoop she has already, depend on it this girl will be both a dwarf and a cripple if we don't put her into stays."

"My child may be a cripple, Ma'am, if such is God's will; but she shall be one of His making, not our's."

All remonstrance was in vain; stays and every species of tight dress were strictly prohibited by the authority of one whose will was, as every man's ought to be, absolute in his own household. He also carefully watched against any evasion of the rule; a riband drawn tightly round my waist would have been cut without hesitation, by his determined

hand; while the little girl of the anxious friend whose operations he had interrupted, enjoyed all the advantages of that system from which I was preserved. She grew up a wand-like figure, graceful and interesting, and died of decline at nineteen, while I, though not able to compare shapes with a wasp or an hour-glass, yet passed muster very fairly among mere human forms, of God's moulding; and I have enjoyed to this hour a rare exemption from headaches, and other lady-like maladies, that appear the almost exclusive privilege of women in the higher classes.

Ungrateful Sons

Many folk tales involve cunning and trickery, but few are more cynically realistic than this. It is impossible to date any folk story accurately, but this one is certainly over 250 years old.

In Winterton lived a rich man named Lacey. As he grew old he decided to give all that he had to his three sons on condition that they should keep him, one this week, one the next, in rotation. Very soon, however, he found that they were fed up with having him around their houses and began to treat him little better than a dog. He consulted an old friend, a lawyer, who explained that he could not get any of his money or property back and that there was only one effective thing he could do.

"Tell me what it is," said the old man, "for I shall starve to death unless you can help."

"Well", said the lawyer, "You have always been a good friend to me, and I shall now be one to you in return. I will lend you a strong chest with a good lock on it, and in it I will put £1,000 in gold pieces. You must pretend to your sons that you have taken it from a safe hiding place, and when you stay with each one in turn you must make a great show of counting the money and rattling it about. You will soon find that they will love you again, and make much of you, and give you as much food and drink as you want."

Lacey did as his friend said, and sure enough his sons grew to love him again, his food was plentiful and his fireplace well stacked with logs.

After a few weeks he took the box back to the lawyer, with profuse and heartfelt thanks, but told his sons that he had hidden it again and would give it to whichever he loved the most when he died. This made them all so careful of his wishes that his last years were lived in peace, plenitude and happiness. On his deathbed he is said to have told them the whole story of the box and forgiven them for their ingratitude.

Man's Other Passion

We all have to eat, and Parson Woodforde went at his food with a will, although sometimes his meals could be interrupted ...

... (Nine guests) came to our House about 3 o'clock and they all dined, supped and spent the Evening, and stayed till 3 o'clock in the Morn with us. We had for Dinner some Pyke and fryed Soals a nice Piece of boiled Beef, Ham and a Couple of Fowls, Peas and Beans, a green Goose rosted, Gooseberry Pies, Currant Tarts, the Charter*, hung Beef scraped &c. For Supper fryed Soals, a Couple of Chicken rosted, cold Ham &c. &c. Artichokes, Tarts &c. Fruit after Dinner and Supper — Strawberries, Cherries, Almonds — Raisins &c. &c ... Just as the Ladies and Gentlemen were going to drink Coffee and Tea in the Garden, I was sent for to go to Weston House to name a Child of Mrs. Custances who was brought to be this Afternoon about 2 o'clock — I therefore walked directly to Weston House and named the Child by name Mary Anne, the smallest Infant I think I ever had in my Arms — The Child came 10 Weeks before its Time, therefore afraid that it would not live. I soon returned to my Company but lost my Coffee and Tea ... (13th July 1785)

No one could cavil at the celebrations that took place when the news arrived that, on 1st August 1798, Norfolk's most famous son had destroyed or captured 11 of the 13 ships-of-the-line of the French Toulon Fleet at the Battle of the Nile.

Great Rejoicings at Norwich today on Lord Nelsons late great & noble Victory over the French near Alexandria in Egypt. An Ox roasted whole in the Market-Place &c ... I gave my Servants this Evening after Supper some strong-Beer and some Punch to drink Admiral Lord Nelson's Health on his late grand Victory and also all the other Officers with him and all the Brave Sailors with them, and also all those brave Admirals, Officers and Sailors that have gained such great and noble Victories of late over the French &c. &c.
(29th November 1798).

*Probably a rich chicken pie.

Home Remedies

Those magnificent meals had their disadvantages, as Woodforde's niece discovered.

Nancy was taken very ill this Afternoon with a pain within her, blown up so as if poisoned, attended with a vomiting. I supposed it proceeded in great measure from what she eat at Dinner and after. She eat for Dinner some boiled Beef rather fat and salt, a good deal of a nice rost duck, and a plenty of boiled Damson Pudding. After Dinner by way of Desert, she eat some greengage Plumbs, some Figgs, and Rasberries and Cream. I desired her to drink a good half pint Glass of warm Rum and Water which she did and soon was a little better — for Supper she had Water-gruel with a couple of small Table Spoonfuls of Rum in it, and going to bed I gave her a good dose of Rhubarb and Ginger. She was much better before she went to bed — And I hope will be brave tomorrow.
(24th September 1790)

In an era when apparently sane, literate people believe in such things as copper bracelets, the Bermuda Triangle and astrology, it ill behoves us to sneer at 'folk' medication, however ineffective it may be.

Mar 11 Friday 1791
Mem. The Stiony on my right Eye-lid still swelled and inflamed very much. As it is commonly said that the Eye-lid being rubbed by the tail of a black Cat would do it much good it not entirely cure it, and having a black Cat, a little before dinner I made a trial of it, and very soon after dinner I found my Eye-lid much abated of the swelling and almost free from Pain. I cannot therefore but conclude it to be of the greatest service to a Stiony on the Eye-lid. Any other Cats Tail may have the above effect in all probability — but I did my Eye-lid with my own black Tom Cat's Tail ...
Mar15 Tuesday 1791
My right Eye again, that is, its Eye-lid much inflamed again and rather painful ...
(Woodforde)

32

Rural Verse Is Down To Earth

A 19th Century Harvest Song

King Arthur was a prudent King,
A prudent King,
A prudent King.
King Arthur was a prudent King,
He bowt five sacks o' barley meal
To make a large pudden.

And a large pudden it was indeed,
And well stuffed with plums,
With great big jobs of suet in,
As big as my two thumbs.

The King and Queen sat down to dine
And all the Court besides;
And what cold fragments they had left,
Next morning they had fried.

The Norfolk Turnippe (18th Century)

Some Countyes vaunte themselves in pyes,
And some in meat excelle;
For turnippes of enormous size
Fair Norfolk bears the belle.

Sport

Country sports have always been fairly bloodthirsty. Bear-baiting has gone and cock and dog fighting are illegal and rare, but many otherwise pleasant people still breed, nurture and guard pheasants and partridges so that they may have the fun of shooting them. It's a sort of upper-crust, rural alternative to getting pissed down the boozer with yer mates and then looking for some other hooligans to fight. Gets rid of one's aggressive instincts, don't y'know. You may well ask why it is more socially acceptable to shoot innocent birds than clout drunken skinheads. I dunno. Parson Woodforde enjoyed his sport, although nowadays his form of fishing is only practised by poachers. Using five men with large nets to drag an entire stretch of river, though effective, is definitely naff today. It's considered much more fun to inveigle a fish into impaling itself on a hook and then to 'fight' it until it collapses from exhaustion. Strange. Funnily enough, most 'sportsmen' dislike cats. It could be that they see uncomfortable parallels with their own behaviour in a cat's habit of playing with its prey. But I think their real objection is to the cat's independence. Hunters and shooters are dog people. They favour large, gooey-eyed, drooling dogs that will bolster their egos by playing Dr. Watson, Robin or Bunny to their owner's Holmes, Batman or Raffles. They too would be reluctant to hang their favourite pointer ...

1781 May 16
Between 7 and 8 o'clock this morning went down to the River a fishing with my Nets...We begun at Lenewade Mill and fished down to Morton. And we had the best day of Fishing we ever had.We caught at one draught only ten Pails of Fish, Pike, Trout and flat fish. The largest Fish we caught was a Pike, which was a Yard long and weighed upwards of thirteen pound after he was brought home. We caught about 20 brace of Pike, but threw back all the small ones — also we caught about 15 brace of Trout, the largest not more than a Pound and half — all the smallest we threw back — 3 brace also of Perch — one tolerable Tench and I dare say near if not quite five hundred Brace of Roach and Dace. Prodigious sport indeed we had today tho' cold and wet.

(The kindly diarist gave away some of the pike and most of the flat fish to the local poor.)

Jan 15 1797 Sunday
We breakfasted, dined, &c. again at home. Mr. Corbould read

Prayers & Preached this afternoon at Weston-Church, he called on us as he went, and told us that one of his Pointer Dogs, by name Tony, was gone mad and had got out in the Night when confined by making a Hole in the door, after loosening his Chain, and went over a great part of the Parish & the Parish of Ling, biting many dogs, Pigs, &c. But was killed this Morning at Mr Corboulds, as he returned home. Mr Corbould hung all his Greyhounds & other Dogs immediately, except a favourite Pointer by name Juno, which is close confined and Antidotes given her, and is to be removed to Bracon, soon. The mischief done by the Dog, as known, is this, 2 Piggs of Mr Howletts, Michael Andrews Yard Dog, Mr. Girlings ditto. 2 Pigs of Cases, and what is worse than all, is, that Jermyn's Son was bit in the hand — so far known, but what other Mischief has been done, God knows. I hope we shall not hear of much more. Mr Corbould is very uneasy about it.

Farms, Fish and Wool

Climate

Arthur Young, in his 'General View of the Agriculture of the County of Norfolk' (1804), had this to say:

There are several points of the compass from which the north and north-east winds blow more directly on this county than on any other in the kingdom: we feel these winds severely in Suffolk; but Norfolk is still more exposed to them, and the climate consequently colder, and more backward in the Spring. Another circumstance which must have some effect on the climate, is the whole western boundary being the fens and marshes of Lincolnshire and Cambridgeshire, to the amount of 5 or 600,000 acres; but this is more likely to affect the salubrity of the air relative to the human body, than to the products of the earth.

Few springs are as cold as that described by Parson Woodforde in 1799.

April 2nd ... Bitter cold again today, hard Frost, but less Wind. There being but few sound Turnips, the poor Stock such as Bullocks, Cows, Sheep &c. are shockingly distressed, few Farmers have scarce anything to give them. Scarce ever known such distressed times for Stock of all kinds, nothing growing, no vegetation, every thing almost dead in the gardens, Beans & Peas &c. almost all gone dead. It is grievous to behold how every Vegetable is hurt — Not even a Daisy or any kind of flower seen. What dismal, dreary Aspect have we at present.

Ode To The North East Wind

Charles Kingsley (1819-1875) took a more positive view of the 'lazy winds' which go through you rather than than round you. Even this extract would be enough to chill his 'Water Babies.'

Welcome, wild North-easter!
    Shame it is to see
Odes to every zephyr;
    Ne'er a verse to thee.
Welcome, black North-easter!
    O'er the German foam;
O'er the Danish moorlands,
    From they frozen home.
Tired we are of summer,
    Tired of gaudy glare,
Showers soft and steaming,
    Hot and breathless air.
Tired of listless dreaming,
    Through the lazy day:
Jovial wind of winter
    Turns us out to play!

. . . .

Come, as came our fathers,
    Heralded by thee,
Conquering from the eastward.
    Lords by land and sea.
Come; and strong within us
    Stir the Viking's blood;
Bracing brain and sinew;
    Blow thow wind of God!

Water

Before the coming of the railway in the second half of the last century, the rivers served as trunk roads. Grain would be taken on small boats from inland ports like Coltishall or Oxborough to Great Yarmouth or King's Lynn, for onward shipment on coasters. Building materials and other goods followed the same routes in reverse. When we regret that the peace of the Broads has been destroyed by modern tourism we should remember that that peace was short-lived: in the early nineteenth century water traffic was constant, although mercifully unmotorised.

NORFOLK is advantageously situated respecting navigation; for of its great circumference of 200 miles, there are but something more than thirty, from Thetford to Bungay, which do not consist of the sea, or of navigable rivers: to the north, the ocean; to the west, the great Ouze; to the east, the sea; to the south, the lesser Ouze, and the Waveney; and, exclusive of this beneficial boundary, the Yare and the Wensum penetrate from Yarmouth to Norwich, and the Bure and Thyrn from the same port to Aylesham. With the last named river the Broads, and their communicating channels in the hundreds of Fleg and Happing, unite and connect the rich district with the sea and with NORWICH, and the advantage is much felt in the conveyance of marle, &c. The navigation of the Nar reaches Narborough, and connects with the Ouze. (Arthur Young)

Daniel Defoe in his 'Tour' (1724) correctly attributed King's Lynn's prosperity to its perfect position in relation to its hinterland.

... We went to Lyn, another rich and populous thriving port-town. It stands on more ground than Yarmouth, and has I think parishes, yet I cannot allow that it has more people than Yarmouth, if so many. It is a beautiful, well built, and well situated town, at the mouth of the River Ouse, and has this particular attending it, which gives it a vast advantage in trade; namely that there is the greatest extent of in-land navigation here, of any port in England, London excepted. The reason whereof is this, that there are more navigable rivers empty themselves here into the sea, including the Washes which are branches of the same port, than at any one mouth of waters in England, except the Thames and the Humber. By these navigable rivers the merchants of Lynn supply about six counties wholly, and three counties in part, with their goods, especially wine and coals, which has given rise to this observation on the town of Lynn, that they bring in more coals, than any sea-port between London and Bristol.

Enclosures

Our rural landscape was created by enclosure, a process that was begun in the late Middle Ages and was not complete until the middle of the nineteenth century. It is a complex subject: ways and means of enclosure differed at different periods, in different soils and in different parts of the country. Broadly speaking, however, enclosure took two principal forms.

The first was the gradual replacement of open fields by smaller, hedged fields. Under the former system farmers owned strips individually in huge fields but, of necessity, decisions about crops and stock had to be taken communally. Enterprising farmers consolidated strips by exchange or purchase, hedged them, and had sole control. This was an expensive business and, as a result, the richer farmers expanded their farms and grew richer and the poor farmers tended to get poorer.

The other important form of enclosure was of common land and this created the greatest resentment, for a peasant with a few small strips could still eke out his precarious living by keeping some stock on the commons, but with the extinction of his common rights he sank to labouring for his wealthier neighbours.

What were the results? On the credit side agriculture became a much more efficient industry: the quality of livestock improved and crop yields increased. On the debit side is the fact that many more people sank than rose and that rural poverty became a serious problem. In the eighteenth century many parishes could not afford to carry out their obligations under the Poor Law. They were allowed to combine with other parishes to build workhouses in which the destitute were, in effect, imprisoned. The workhouses were hired out to manufacturers who obtained cheap labour in return for keeping the unfortunate inmates alive. (Proponents of a modernised version of this efficient system call it Workfare.) The new capitalists in the burgeoning cities of the Industrial Revolution had no problem recruiting labour, for the dispossessed rural poor found life in the vilest, disease-ridden slum preferable to the slavery of the workhouse.

Two passages, both from 1549, say all there is to be said about the enclosures from the point of view of the smallholders. The first is from the manifesto produced by the rebels under Robert Kett, who gathered on Mousehold Heath. There they organised the repossession of common land which had been enclosed and lived on the flocks and herds of the landlords. The authorities, in the form of the Earl of Warwick, put down the rebellion and, if the figures can be believed, killed 3,000 of the 6,000 insurgents. Robert Kett was hung from a gibbet at Norwich Castle, his brother William from the west tower of Wymondham Abbey.

41

The present condition of possessing land seemeth miserable and slavish-holding it all at the pleasure of great men; not freely, but by prescription, and, as it were, at the will and pleasure of the lord . . . The lands which in the memory of our fathers were common, those are ditched and hedged and made several; the pastures are enclosed and we are shut out.

A sermon by Bishop Hugh Latimer demonstrates that the Church of England did not always side with 'the great and the good.' It is interesting to note that he regarded unemployment as a slur on the King's honour.

"You landlords, you rent-raisers . . . you have for your possession yearly too much . . . It is the King's honour that the commonwealth be advanced, that the dearth be provided for, and the commodities of this realm so employed, as it may be to the setting of his subjects on work and keeping them from idleness. If the King's honour, as some may say, standeth in the great multitude of the people, then these graziers, enclosers and rent-raisers are hinderers of the King's honour; for whereas have been a great many householders and inhabitants, there is now but a shepherd and his dog. My lords and masters, such proceedings do intend plainly to make of the yeomanry slavery."

The Advantages Of Enclosure

Arthur Young put the efficiency argument 250 years later, at the peak of the Agrarian Revolution which had made Norfolk farmers and landlords, especially Thomas Coke of Holkham, famous throughout Europe. The 'wastes' he refers to were, of course, commons which by 1844 had shrunk to only 27,000 acres. Our modern landscape of individually hedged fields had been created. Before the improvements of the 18th century the countryside was far more open than it is today, even after the recent removal of so many hedges.

'The size of farms is a subject upon which so much has been written, that to enter into a discussion on the subject in the Report of a single county, would be to swell a book with general subjects, which ought to be appropriated to local and particular ones. I shall only observe, that the vast improvements which have been made in Norfolk, by converting boundless heaths, sheep-walks and warrens, into well-cultivated districts, by enclosing and marling, are such as were never yet made by small farmers. Great farmers have converted in this county three or four hundred thousand acres of wastes in to gardens: can any thing therefore be so grossly absurd, as to find fault with such divisions of the earth as have produced these effects? Little farmers have never, in any county that I am acquainted with, produced equal effects: ...

The Norfolk farmers are famous for their great improvements, the excellency of their management, and the hospitable manner in which they live and receive their friends, and all strangers that visit the county. I have on various occasions found how well they merit their reputation.

An Early Ecologist

Efficiency had its drawbacks, as Mr Johnson of Thurning told Arthur Young. This farmer was obviously a careful observer of wildlife.

I cannot but notice two growing evils with us, of which but little notice is taken:—
1st, the number of insects in the lands, owing to the loss of rooks, by felling so many rookeries, and not taking care of what are left; 2d, the increase of mice, and, were I to give my opinion as to the quantity and damage done, but few would give credit to it: I have, at different times, had five mice killed to every coomb of corn moved off the stacks in the summer season, and sometimes double that quantity; besides being on every other part of the premises corn and grass pieces not excepted. Some are driven into the barns and stacks in wet seasons; but when the wheat stands long on the shock, we are sure to have most mice in our barns and stacks, except where they are driven away by some other vermin:—

in my memory there were 20 grey owls, where there are now one, and though the country was in a rougher state, we had not so many mice, the owls prey very much on them, and in wet weather they are more exposed to the owl than to any other vermin. The grey owl is destroyed by the game-keepers, and by felling the pollards. I have seen a young hare in their nests, but never saw a young pheasant or partridge:— the white, or church owl, are not so destructive to game; and were there places made within the top of one end of every barn, like a box, for them to pass through as they come into the barn, they would there make their nests, and become more numerous, and be of great service.

Note: The white, or church owl could only be the barn owl. The grey owl must be what we now call the tawny owl.

Hard Times

Life for an agricultural worker was always hard. Sometimes it became virtually unbearable, as George Edwards recalled. He was the son of a farm labourer and grew up to take an active part in the new Agricultural Workers Union. He became Labour M.P. for S.W.Norfolk in 1922.

'At the time of my birth (Oct 5) my father was again a bullock feeder, working seven days a week, leaving home in the morning before it was light, and not returning in the evening until it was dark. He never saw his children at this time, except for a little while on Sunday, as they were always put to bed during the winter months before his return from work. The condition of the the family grew worse, for, although the Corn Laws were repealed in 1849, the price of food did not decrease to any great extent, but wages did go down. Married men's wages were reduced from 9s. to 8s. per week, and single men's wages from 7s. to 6s. per week. It was the rule in those days that the single men should work for 2s. per week less than the married men. Before the repeal of the Corn Laws had the effect of reducing the cost of living to any great extent, the great Crimean War broke out. This it will be remembered was in 1854. Food rose to famine prices. The price of bread went up to 1s. per 4lb loaf, sugar to 8d. per lb., tea to 6d. per oz., in fact, every article of food rose to almost prohibitive figures ...

I was then four years of age, and the hardships of those days will never be erased from my memory, My father's wages were not sufficient to buy bread alone for the family by 4s. per week. My eldest brother

Joseph, who was twelve years old, was at work for 1s. 6d. per week, my second brother John, ten years old, was working for 1s. 2d. per week.'

(During this period his father was imprisoned for stealing three turnips. When he was released, as he had no job, the family was sent to the workhouse. Luckily there was a happy ending, for he managed to get a job making bricks and the family returned to their cottage.)

Parson Woodforde had visited a workhouse in March 1781 ...

We dined at 3 o'clock and after we had smoked a Pipe etc., we took a ride to the House of Industry about 2 miles West of Dereham, and a very large building at present tho' there wants another Wing. About 380 Poor in it now, but they didn't look either healthy or cheerful, a great number die there, 27 have died since Christmas last.

Techniques and Technicalities

When Arthur Young was writing — in 1804 — the Industrial Revolution's main agricultural effect had been on demand. The country's population had doubled in the previous century (to about 11 million) and a large proportion were in the industrial cities, although it was not until after 1830 that the urban population equalled the rural. Obviously mechanisation was creeping in: drilling was common but the old method of planting seeds by hand, called dibbling, still had its devotees in spite of its unfortunate effect on the supply of maid-servants ...

Mr BURTON, of Langley, remarked, that good as this practice was in some respects for the poor, there are inconveniences flowing from it. Girls, old enough for service, are kept at home by it. Gleaning is their employment in harvest, which gives them idle habits in the fields, then dibbling follows; and the girls lying about under hedges with men, produces the natural consequences on their manners; bastardy flourishes, and maid-servants are uncommonly scarce.

Mr JOHNSON, of Thurning, makes the same observation on the ill effects of dibbling as Mr BURTON. The great girls do not drop so well as children, nor is the work so well done as formerly: they now drop between the forefinger and the thumb, which is much inferior to doing it between the fore and middle finger.

Young was an enthusiast for efficiency, as this passage on the arrival of the future in Heydon shows. The village is now one of the most peaceful in Norfolk: it is difficult to imagine it resounding to the puffings and clangings of a mighty engine.

The first steam-engine erected in Norfolk for merely agricultural purposes, and for what I know, in England, is one now erecting at Haydon by Colonel BULLER. He has contracted for the sum of 600 l. It is to do the work of ten horses; to work a threshing mill that shall thresh and dress six lasts a day: it is to grind corn also, and cut straw; to grind nine bushels of wheat with one bushel of good Newcastle coals, of 84 lb weight, and this with all the other works going on at the same time: the Colonel to find timber. Last year his hay and straw cutting cost above 70 l. therefore little doubt can be entertained of the plan answering.

Note: £600 was a considerable capital investment in 1804. A farm labourer earned about £30.00 per year and would have paid some £2.50 p.a. out of it in rent for his tied cottage. That small, basic dwelling would have cost the farmer between £100 and £150 to build.

Poultry

Rearing poultry on a large scale has long been a local industry. Daniel Defoe described the flocks being driven to London in his 'Tour Through the Whole Island of Great Britain' (1724).

... This county of Suffolk is particularly famous for furnishing the city of London and all the counties round, with turkeys; and, it is thought, there are more turkeys bred in this county, and the part of Norfolk that adjoins to it, than in all the rest of England, especially for sale. Nor will it be found so inconsiderable an article as some may imagine, if this be true which I received an account of from a person living on the place, (viz.) that they have counted 300 droves of turkeys (for they drive them all in droves on foot) pass in one season over Stratford-Bridge on the River Stour, on the road from Ipswich to London. These droves, as they say, generally contain from three hundred to a thousand each drove; so that one may suppose them to contain 500 one with another, which is 150,000 in all; and yet this is one of the least passages, the numbers which travel by New Market-Heath, and the open country and the forest, and also by Sudbury and Clare, being many more.

For the further supplies of the markets of London with poultry, of which these countries particularly abound: they have within these few years found it practicable to make the geese travel on foot too, as well as the turkeys; and a prodigious number are brought up to London in droves from the farthest parts of Norfolk. They begin to drive them generally in August, by which time the harvest is almost over, and the geese may feed in the stubbles as they go. Thus they hold on to the end of October, when the roads begin to be too stiff and deep for their broad feet and short legs to march in. Besides these methods of driving these creatures on foot, they have of late also invented a new method of carriage, being carts formed on purpose, with four stories or stages, to put the creatures in one above another, by which invention one cart will carry a very great number and for the smoother going, they drive with two horses a-breast, like a coach, so quartering the road for the ease of the gentry that thus ride: changing horses they travel night and day; so that they bring the fowls 70, 80 or 100 miles in two days and one night.

Livestock

The fattening of cattle driven from Scotland and Northern England was the most important agricultural activity in Norfolk's marshy areas for centuries. The best known market for these store cattle was St. Faith's, north of Norwich.

In this vast tract of meadows are fed a prodigious number of black cattle, which are said to be fed up for the fattest beef, though not the largest in England; and the quantity is so great, as that they not only supply the city of Norwich, the town of Yarmouth, and county adjacent, but send great quantities of them weekly in all the winter season, to London. And this in particular is worthy of remark, that the gross of all the Scots cattle which come yearly into England, are brought hither, being brought to a small village lying north of the city of Norwich, called St Faiths, where the Norfolk graziers go and buy them.

These scots runts, so they call them, coming out of the cold and barren mountains in the Highlands of Scotland feed so eagerly on the

rich pasture in these marshes, that they thrive in an unusual manner, and grow monstrously fat; and the beef is so delicious for taste, that the inhabitants prefer 'em to the English cattle, which are much larger and fairer to look at. Some have told me there are above 40,000 of these Scots cattle fed in this country every year, and most of them in the said marshes between Norwich, Beccles and Yarmouth.
(Daniel Defoe, 1724)

But wool, whether raw or in the form of cloth, was Norfolk's most important product. Much of the North West corner was open sheep-walk until the middle of the 18th century, but the 'golden hoof' also trod the coastal marshes which had been protected from flooding from at least the Middle Ages.

'Item, that a warrant be made to help shut up and make the sea banks before the pastures of Tychewell that at high springs the sea breaketh in to the pastures and destroyeth the pasture and also bringeth the salt sands amongst the grass and maketh it bitter, that the sheep will not feed them upon it...'
(Paston Letters, 1470)

The village of Worstead gave its name to a cloth of which Norfolkmen were proud. John Paston writes to his wife Margaret in September 1465...

'...I pray you ye will send me hither two eln of worsted for doublets to hap me this cold winter, and that ye inquire where William Paston bought his tippet of fine worsted which is almost like silk; and if that be much finer than that ye should buy me after 7 or 8s., then buy me a quarter and the nail thereof for collars, though it be dearer than the other, for I would make my doublet all worsted for worship of Norfolk..'

Wool

The spinning of wool was a cottage industry until the Industrial Revolution. In the villages of south and east Norfolk, the whirr of the spinning wheel must have been as familiar a sound as the swish of a scythe. The rural outworkers were paid by the merchants who financed the cloth industry from raw wool to finished bales. They were our first capitalists and they began to flourish in the late Middle Ages. Growth was rapid: English exports of 'cloths of assize' rose from around 20,000 p.a. in the second half of the 14th century to over 100,000 by 1540. Exports of raw wool dropped proportionately. Defoe found the industry still flourishing in the early eighteenth century.

When we come into Norfolk, we see a face of diligence spread over the whole country; the vast manufactures carried on (in chief) by the Norwich weavers, employs all the country round in spinning yarn for them; besides many thousand packs of yarn which they receive from other countries, even from as far as Yorkshire, and Westmoreland ... This side of Norfolk is very populous, and thronged with great and spacious market-towns, more and larger than any other part of England so far from London, except Devonshire, and the West-riding of Yorkshire; for example, between the frontiers of Suffolk and the city of Norwich on this side, which is not above 22 miles in breadth, are the following market-towns, viz.

Thetford,	Hingham,	Harleston,
Dis,	West Deerham,	East Deerham,
Harling,	Attleboro',	Watton,
Bucknam,	Windham,	Loddon, &c.

Most of these towns are very populous and large; but that which is most remarkable is, that the whole country round them is so interspersed with villages, and those villages so large, and so full of people, that they are equal to market-towns in other counties. An eminent weaver of Norwich, gave me a scheme of their trade on this occasion, by which, calculating from the number of looms at that time employed in the city of Norwich only, besides those employed in other towns in the same county, he made it appear very plain, that there were 120000 people employed in the woollen and silk manufactures of that city only, not that the people all lived in the city too: but I say, they were employed for spinning the yarn used for such goods as were all made in that city.

This shows the wonderful extent of the Norfolk manufacture, or stuff-weaving trade, by which so many thousands of families are maintained.

Elizabethan Poverty

The workers who actually spun and wove were not necessarily prosperous. These few extracts from the Norwich Census of the Poor of 1570 show that what we now call single-parent families have always been among the poorest members of our society. (Presumably Anne Barwic travelled daily for her husband in order to feed him. Prisoners then who had no money to buy food, or friends or relatives to provide it, slowly starved to death on the inadequate diet they received.)

Alice Reade, the wyfe of Robert Coke, reder, by whom she hath had 2 sons, the eldest 9 yeris olde, which she set to spynnyng; and Jone Rede of 14 yeris that spyn mydle worp. The same Alice is 40 yer olde & hyr husbond hath left hyr with the 3 children aforsyd & a sukyng child without help, & is run awaye, & had a wyfe befor, & have dwelt here a 5 yeris, & she spyn wolle.

Robert Barwic of the age of 60 yere, that is & hath been in pryson for dett, & Anne, his wyfe, of 40 yeris, that hath no exercise butt traveyle dayelye in hir husbondes behalfe; & hath at their charge 8 children, all ydle, and lyve upon the labour of others, and the bygest of them kepe the bowlynge alye.

Jone, the wyfe of Thomas Burges, gon from hyr a 4 yere paste she know not wher, of the age of 40 yeres, a spinster of Duch worke; a son & daughter, the eldest of 8 yeris which knytt, & hath dwelt here all hyr lyfe.

William Stevenson ... of 46 yeris, dornek weaver not in worke, & Jane, his wyfe, of 42 yers, that spyn white warpe; & a child of 14 yers that knytt gret hose by whom come theyr cheyfe lyvinge, & have dwelt here ever.

Shipping

The importance of the sea in the past as a highway for goods cannot be overstated. In Norfolk, it wasn't just King's Lynn and Yarmouth that throve, but also all the little ports along the North coast. Coal came in from Newcastle, wood from the Baltic; wool was shipped to Flanders and corn to London. Fishing was important too: in the early 17th century there were over 200 local fishing boats in Yarmouth and at the time of the autumn herring fishing over 600 ships might shelter in the harbour when conditions were too stormy to fish. Even in the Middle Ages, ships sailed from Cley and Wiveton to fish off Iceland. Landowners with their own ships, or the money to hire transport, could send their produce to the best markets. Here, John Paston I is advised of the state of the malt market in 1462 ...

And as for the price here, at Yarmouth, one quarter with every bushel level in the combes is worth 2s. 2d. and no better now. It was worth 2/6d. But I hear tell it is good in London, for there I understand is best sale. I can think it shall fall here, for the fields are reasonably fair here in Flegg, and so up to Norwich; one quarter carried from Yarmouth to London will cost you 6d.

The great men of the time did not feel that trade was beneath them: rather the opposite. In 1490 John Sherwood, Bishop of Durham, wrote to John Paston III ...

Foreasmuch as I have coals and other things in these parts, and also ye have in those parts corn, wine and wax, and as I am informed that ye be not evil willed to deal with me, no more than I am to deal with you, in uttering and receiving of such things, the which might be to the profit of us both, I therefore send unto you ... William Walker, gentleman usher of my chamber, to commune with you herein, so that by deliberation such a way may be taken in this behalf as may be to the profit of either of us.

A Successful Farmer

In 1804 this tenant of a large farm on the Holkham Estate thought of his ship as a modern farmer thinks of his lorry. He was obviously a far cry from the popular image of the turnip-brained farmer whose only contact with the outside world is a weekly visit to the local market!

Mr. OVERMAN, of Burnham, has a small ship, which he keeps constantly employed in carrying his corn to London, in bringing rape-cake for manure from Holland, London, Hull, or wherever it is to be procured best, and at the cheapest rate. When his farm does not in this manner produce employment, he sends her for coals, or deals, or on any service which times and markets render eligible: and this speculation answers well. He conceives that drilled corn, kept perfectly clean, is a better sample than the common run of broadcast, and he finds it difficult to get, in the country, a price proportioned to the merit of his productions, and to send the corn by sea to London, does not cost so much as land-carriage to Lynn would do. Entering on a new farm of Mr Coke's, a year and a half past, and finding many hurdles necessary, he sent his ship to Sussex for a lading of hurdles: there made much better, of riven oak, and at the same time lighter than others to be had in Norfolk, they cost him 3s.6d. each, and will last 20 years.
(Arthur Young)

The Red Herring For Yarmouth

For centuries Great Yarmouth deserved its name, for it was one of the most important fishing ports in Northern Europe, but over-fishing of the herring in this century killed the industry. John Speed, writing in 1611, said 'there is yearly in September the worthiest Herring Fishery in Europe ... which maketh the Town much richer all the year following, but very unsavoury for the time.' *Sir Thomas Browne described it. (A shotten herring is one that has spawned, and therefore has no roe.)*

Of Herring incredible shoales passe by this coast about 7 September untill towards the end of October when their shoals move more southward. Unto this fishing boats resort from the north and west country, from the Low Countries & some from France wh. bring in herrings into Yarmouth. Such store sometimes is taken in a day that..that is above an herring for every man in England. Tis observed that in an east or northeast wind they grow shotten, butt the wind changing in a day or two grow full agayne. In their descent from the north they passe not into the bay of Lyne or the south shoare of Norfolk, butt passe beyond the poynt of Cromer. Nothing is found in their bellies, & dye immediately out of the water. The greatest part being salted & hang upon sticks in howses for the purpose & so gently smoake and dryed by a great furnace especiall of Ash ... This citty is obliged by charter to send unto his Majestie yearly Herring pyes; each contains 3 herrings wch is duly observed.

Most of the herrings hanging in the smokehouses became red herrings: saltier and drier than kippers and bloaters, they kept well for months. (The expression 'a red herring' is a contraction of ' to draw a red herring'. A red herring drawn across the scent of a fox will distract the hounds.) Thomas Nashe (1567-1601) told the unlikely story of the discovery of this delicacy.

A Fisherman of Yarmouth, hauing drawne so many herrings he wist not what to do withall, hung the residue that he could not sel...in the sooty roofe of his shad a drying ... The weather was colde, and good fires hee kept...and what with his fiering and smoking, or smokie firing, in that his narrow lobby, his herrings, which were as white as whales bone when hee hung them up, now lookt as red as a lobster. It was foure or fiue days before either hee or his wife espied it, & when they espied it, they fell downe on their knees and blessed themslus, & cride, a miracle, a miracle & with proclaiming it among their neighbours they could not be content, but to the court the fisherman would, and present it to the King, then lying at *Burrough* Castle two mile off ... Saint Denis for Fraunce, Saint James for Spaine, Saint Patrick for Ireland, Saint George for England, and the red Herring for Yarmouth.

Yarmouth was much more than a simple fishing port.

But this is only one branch of the great trade carried on in this town. Another part of this commerce, is in the exporting these herrings after they are cured; and for this their merchants have a great trade to Genoa, Leghorn, Naples, Messina and Venice as also to Spain and Portugal also exporting with their herring very great quantities of worsted stuffs made of silk and worsted; camblets, &c. the manufactures of the neighbouring city of Norwich, and the places adjacent. Besides this, they carry on a very considerable trade with Holland, whose opposite neighbours they are; and a vast quantity of woollen manufactures they export to the Dutch every year. They have also a considerable trade to Norwich, and to the Baltic, from whence they bring back deals, and fir-timber, oaken plank, baulks, spar, oars, pitch, tar, hemp, flax, spruce canvas, and sail-cloth; with all manner of naval stores, which they generally have a consumption for in their own port, where they build a very great number of ships every year, besides re-fitting and repairing the old. Add to this the coal trade between Newcastle and the river of Thames, in which they are so improved of late years, that they have now a greater share of it than any other town in England.

For the carrying on all these trades, they must have a very great number of ships, either of their own, or employed by them; and it may be some measure be judged of by this, that in the year 1697, I had an account from the town register, that there was then 1,123 sail of ships using the sea, and belonged to the town, besides such ships as the merchants of Yarmouth might be concerned in, and be part-owners of, belonging to other ports.

(Daniel Defoe 1724)

James Woodforde visited the town in September 1776 ...

We got to Yarmouth about 4 o'clock, and there we dined, supped and slept at the Wrestlers in Church Square kept by one Orton. A very good house. After we dined we took a walk on the Quay and viewed the Dutch vessells, about 70 sail which came in last night, to go a-fishing soon for Herrings. The Dutch are very droll fellows to look at, strange, heavy, bad dressed People with monstrous large Trousers, and many with wooden shoes ...

After breakfast we each took a Yarmouth coach and drove down upon the coast ... It was very pleasant and delightful indeed. Nothing can beat what we saw today — immense sea Room, Shipps and Boats passing and repassing — the Wind being rather high, the Waves like Mountains coming into the Shore ... In the evening we took a walk on the Quay, as fine a one as ever was seen. A great deal of company walking backward and forward. We got on board an English vessel, and were treated with Wine, Gin, etc. The sailors behaved very civil indeed to us, had a difficult Matter to make them take anything, but at last I did, and all the silver I had, being only ... 0. 1. 0. She was a Collier and going soon back to Sunderland.

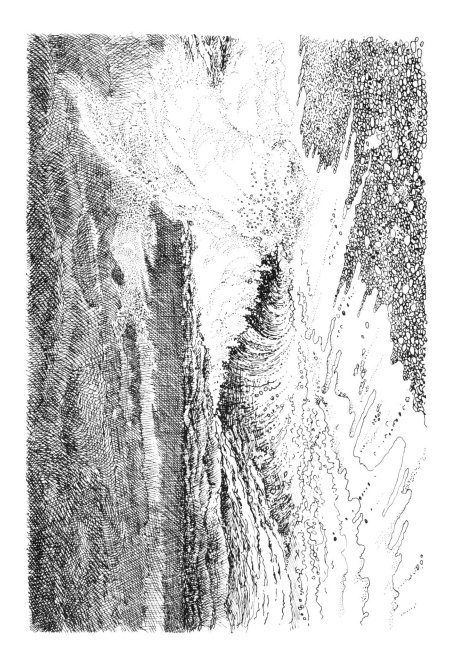

Shipwreck

The Norfolk coast, though extensive, has few harbours that are easily accessible in bad weather: the north-east corner has none. Defoe described what this could mean to the sailors and the beachcombers.

From Yarmouth I resolved to pursue my first design, (viz.) to view the sea-side on this coast, which is particularly famous for being one of the most dangerous and most fatal to the sailors in all England, I may say in all Britain; and the more so, because of the great number of ships which are continually going and coming this way, in their passage between London and all the northern coasts of Great-Britain . . .

As I went by land from Yarmouth northward, along the shore towards Cromer aforesaid, and was not then fully master of the reason of these things, I was surprised to see, in all the way from Winterton, that the farmers, and country people had scarce a barn, or a shed, or a stable; nay, not the pales of their yards, and gardens, not a hogsty, not a necessary-house, but what was built of old planks, beams, wales and timbers, &c. the wrecks of ships, and ruin of mariners' and merchants' fortunes.

About the year 1692, (I think it was that year) there was a melancholy example of what I have said of this place; a fleet of 200 sail of light colliers (so they call the ships bound northward empty to fetch coals from Newcastle to London) went out of Yarmouth Roads with a fair wind, to pursue their voyage, and were taken short with a storm of wind at N.E. after they were past Winterton Ness, a few leagues; some of them, whose masters were a little more wary than the rest, tacked, and put back in time, and got safe into the roads; but the rest pushing on, in hopes to keep out to sea, and weather it, were by the violence of the storm driven back, when they were too far embayed to weather Winterton Ness, as above; and so were forced to run west, every one shifting for themselves, as well as they could. Some run away for Lyn Deeps but few of them, (the night being so dark) could find their way in there; some but very few rid it out, at a distance; the rest being above 140 sail were all driven on shore, and dashed to pieces, and very few of the people on board were saved. At the very same unhappy juncture, a fleet of loaden ships were coming from the north, and being just crossing the same bay, were forcibly driven into it, not able to weather the Ness, and so were involved in the same ruin as the light fleet was; also some coasting vessels loaden with corn from Lyn, and Wells, and bound for Holland, were with the same unhappy luck just come out, to begin their voyage, and some of them lay at anchor; these also met with the same misfortune, so that in the whole, above 200 sail of ships, and above a thousand people perished in the disaster of that one miserable night, very few escaping.

Mainly Illegal

The Peasant's Revolt

Jean Froissart was born in the late 1330's and at different times was attached to the royal households of both England and France. His Chronicles remain an important source of information on the fourteenth century. He wrote in considerable detail about the Peasant's Revolt of 1381 when 'the evil-disposed began to rise, saying they were too severely oppressed; that at the beginning of the world there were no slaves, and no one ought to be treated as such unless he had committed treason against his lord as Lucifer had done against God; but they had done no such thing, for they were neither angels nor spirits, but men formed after the same likeness with their lords, who treated them as beasts.' *Froissart himself had no sympathy with these ideas. This extract concerns a large band of peasants from Lincolnshire, Norfolk and Suffolk who were marching to London under the leadership of William Lister. (Medieval chroniclers habitually exaggerated the numbers in crowds and armies tenfold or more.)*

In their road they stopped near Norwich, and forced everyone to join them, so that none of the common people remained behind. The reason why they stopped near Norwich was that the governor of the town was a knight called Sir Robert Salle: he was not by birth a gentleman, but, having acquired great renown for his ability and courage, King Edward had created him a knight. He was the strongest and most handsome man in England. Lister and his companions took it into their heads that they would make this knight their commander, and carry him with them, in order to be the more feared. They sent orders to him to come out into the fields to speak with them, or they would attack and burn the city. The knight, considering it was much better for him to go to them than that they should commit such outrages, mounted his horse and went out of the town alone to hear what they had to say. When they perceived him coming they showed him every mark of respect, and courteously entreated him to dismount and talk with them. He did dismount, and committed a great folly; for when he had so done, having surrounded him, they at first conversed in a friendly way, saying, "Robert, you are a knight, and a man of great weight in this country, renowned for your valour; yet, notwithstanding all this, we know who you are; you are not a gentleman, but the son of a poor mason, just such as ourselves. Do you come with us, as our commander, and we will make so great a lord of you that one quarter of England shall be under your command."

The knight, on hearing them thus speak, was exceedingly angry; he would never have consented to such a proposal; and, eyeing them with inflamed looks, answered, "Begone, wicked scoundrels and false traitors as you are! Would you have me desert my natural lord for such a company of knaves as you? Would you have me dishonour myself? I would much rather you were all hanged, for that must be your end." On saying this, he attempted to mount his horse; but, his foot slipping from the stirrup, his horse took fright. They then shouted and cried, "Put him to death!" When he heard this he let his horse go and, drawing a handsome Bordeaux sword, he began to skirmish, and soon cleared the crowd from about him, that it was a pleasure to see. Some attempted to close with him; but with each stroke he gave he cut off heads, arms, feet or legs. There were none so bold but were afraid; and Sir Robert that day performed marvellous feats of arms. These wretches were upward of forty thousand; they shot and flung at him such things that, had he been clothed in steel instead of being unarmoured, he must have been overpowered: however he killed twelve of them, besides many whom he wounded. At last he was overthrown, when they cut off his legs and arms and rent his body in piecemeal. Thus ended Sir Robert Salle, which was a great pity; and when the knights and squires of England heard of it they were much enraged.'

(The 'unbridled and insolent' Henry Despenser, Bishop of Norwich, drove the rebels from the city and defeated them at North Walsham Heath. Lister took refuge in North Walsham church but was dragged out and drawn and quartered.)

An Assault

The rising great men of Norfolk behaved in the 15th century like Chicago gangsters, intimidating juries with bands of armed men, and allowed no scruples to interfere with their ambition. The Wymondham here is John Wymondham, the first of his family to acquire Felbrigg. James Gloys was family chaplain to the Pastons and also frequently acted as a man of business for the family, especially for Margaret who wrote this letter in 1448 to her husband John Paston I. Men of the cloth needed also to be men of resource ...

'Right worshipful husband, I recommend me to you and pray to weet that on Friday last passed before noon, the parson of Oxnead being at mass in our parish church*, even at the levation of the sacring, James Gloys had been in the town and came homeward by Wymondham's gate. And Wymondham stood at his gate and John Norwood his man stood by him and Thomas Hawes his other man stood in the street by the cannel side. And James Gloys came with his hat on his head between both his men, as he was wont of custom to do. And when Gloys was against Wymondham he said thus. "Cover thy head!" And Gloys said again, "So I shall for thee." And when Gloys was further passed by the space of three or four strides, Wymondham drew out his dagger and said, "Shalt thou so, knave?" And therewith Gloys turned him and drew out his dagger and defended him, fleeing into my mother's place; and Wymondham and his man Hawes cast stones and drove Gloys into my mother's place. And Hawes followed into my mother's place and cast a stone as much as a farthing loaf into the hall after Gloys; and ran out of the place again. And Gloys followed out and stood without the gate, and then Wymondham called Gloys thief and said he should die, and Gloys said he lied and called him churl, and bade him come himself or else the best man he had, and Gloys would answer him one for one. And then Hawes ran into Wymondham's place and fetched a spear and a sword, and took his master his sword. And with the noise of this assault and affray my mother and I came out of the church from the sacring; and I bade Gloys go into my mother's place again, and so he did. And then Wymondham called my mother and me strong whores ... When Wymondham said that James should die I said to him that I supposed that he should repent him if he slew him or did him any bodily harm; and he said

Margaret Paston was staying in her Norwich house.

61

nay, he should never repent him nor have a farthing worth of harm though he killed you and him both. And I said yes, and he slew the least child that belongeth to your kitchen, and if he did he were like, I suppose, to die for him. It is told me that he shall come to London in haste. I pray you beware how ye walk if he be there, for he is full cursed-hearted and malicious. I wot well he will not set upon you manly, but I believe he will start upon you or on some of your men like a thief.'

Robbery With Violence

This petition of c.1454 from the Paston papers tells the story of a felonious thug, or was he a local Robin Hood?

'These be divers of the riots and offences done in the hundred of Blofeld in the county of Norffolk, and in other towns by Robert Lethum, otherwise called Robert Ledham of Wytton by Blofeld ...

Many persons know and unknown the said Robert Ledham kept at his house in the manner of a fortress and issued out at their pleasure and at his desire ... sometimes 6, sometimes 12 and sometimes 30 or more, armed, jakked* and helmeted, with bows and arrows, spears and halberds, and rode over the country and oppressed the King's people, and did many horrible and abominable deeds ...

On the Monday next before Easter Day ... 10 rioters, with a brother of the wife of the said Robert Lethum, lay in wait in the highway under Thorpe wood upon Philip Berney, esquire, and his man coming from the shire, and shot at him and smote the horse of the said Philip with arrows, and then overrode him and took him and beat him and robbed him ...

3 of the said riotous fellowship, the same day, year and place, lay in wait upon Edmond Brown, gentleman, and with naked swords and other weapons fought with him for the space of quarter of an hour, and took and robbed him ...

... On the Monday next after Easter Day the same year, took from one John Wilton 4 head of cattle ... and killed them and laid them in salt and afterwards eat them.

In like wise the said Robert Lethum and his men assaulted John Coke of Witton, breaking down his doors at 11 of the clock in the night;

*jack: a heavy, protective, leather jerkin.

and with their swords maimed him and gave him 7 great wounds and took from him certain goods and chattells . . . and they beat the mother of the same John Coke, and smote her upon the crowne of her head with a sword; of the which hurt she might never be healed unto the day of her death.

(The catalogue of theft and mayhem continues, the robbers even attacking a parson in his church where they 'brake his hede in his owyn chauncell'.)

The said Robert Lethum, with his said riotous fellowship . . . . made so many riots in the hundred where he dwells that divers and many gentlemen, franklins, and good men durst not abide in their manors neither ride nor walk about their occupations without more persons arrayed in manner and form of war attending and waiting on them than their livelihood would extend to. And so, for the safety of their lives and in eschewing such inordinate costs as never was seen in that county before, many of them forsook and left their own habitation, wife and child, and drew to fortresses and good towns for that time: . . . to Caister . . . Norwich . . . Saint Benet's . . . Aylesham . . . Much Yarmouth.

Notwithstanding that the livelihood the said Ledham hath passeth not £20.00 . . . (he) yet keepeth in his house daily 20 men, besides women and great multitude of such unruly people as have resorted to him . . . to which he giveth clothing, and yet beside that he giveth to other men that be not dwelling in his household. And of the said 20 men, not seven are occupied with husbandry; and all they that use husbandry, as well as the others, go jakked and helmeted ready for war, which in this country is thought right strange.'

More Rural Crime

In the eighteenth century there were over 200 offences for which the death penalty could be imposed although, in practice, it was rarely exacted for minor offences. Parson Woodforde noted in his diary in 1783 that . . .

The two Fellows who were suspected breaking open my Stable and many others, were tried this Day at the Sessions at Norwich and convicted of the Robbery of stealing a Sack from Mr. Howlett and are to remain in Prison for three years — which I hope will do good.

Early in the next century the savagery of the laws was reduced:
pickpockets were transported to Australia for life instead of being hanged,
and by 1832 even such heinous offences as sheep-stealing and housebreak-
ing were no longer punishable by execution. But the man whose hanging
was mentioned by Woodforde in March 1785 would have stood a good chance
of receiving the same penalty until quite recently . . .

... At the Assizes at Thetford in this County 8 Prisoners were
condemned, three of the above were reprieved. — The other five left
for execution . . . Js Cliffen . . . was hanged on Thursday last at Norwich on Castle Hill and behaved most daring audacious — His crime
was robbing 2 old Men, Brothers, by names Seaman on the Yaxham

Road, knocked them both down first, of which Blows one of them died soon after — the other recovered. Cliffen's body was this day carried to Badley Moor and there hung in Chains at one Corner of the said Moor.

Danger From The Sea

In 1450 the War with France was still going on. Margaret Paston wrote in March that ...

There been many enemies against Yarmouth and Cromer, and have done much harm and taken many Englishmen and put them in great distress and greatly ransomed them.

Presumably one of these raiding parties was responsible for the outrages noted by Agnes Paston. The pilgrims in question were probably on their way to Bacton, or Broomholm, Priory. It is interesting to see that, although the Hundred Years War was often pretty savage, robbing pilgrims was 'out of order'.

'Richard Lynsted came this day from Paston, and let me weet that on Saturday last past Drawale, half brother to Waryn Harman, was taken with enemies walking by the sea side and have him forth with them; and they took 2 pilgrims, a man and a woman, and they robbed the woman and let her go and lead the man to the sea, and when they knew he was a pilgrim they gave him money and set him again on the land. And they have this week taken 4 vessels of Wyntyrton and Happysborough, and Ecles men been sore afraid for taking of more, for there been 10 great vessels of the enemy's. God give grace that the sea may be better kept than it is now, or else it shall be a perylous dwellyng by the sea coast.'

Piracy

This inscription from the churchyard of St Nicholas, Great Yarmouth, tells its own story.

To
The Memory of
DAVID BARTLEMAN
Master of the Brig Alexander & Margaret
Of North Shields
Who on the 31st Jan 1781 on the Norfolk Coast
With only three 8 Pounders and ten Men and Boys
Nobly defended himself
Against a Cutter carrying eighteen 4 pounders
And upwards of a Hundred Men
Commanded by the notorious English Pirate
FALL
and fairly beat him off
Two hours after the Enemy came down upon him again
When totally disabled his Mate Daniel MacAuley
Expiring with the loss of blood
And himself dangerously wounded
He was obliged to strike and ransome
He brought his shattered Vessel into Yarmouth
With more
Than the Honours of a Conqueror
And died here in consequence of his wounds
On the 14th February following
In the 25th Year of his Age
To commemorate the Gallantry of his Son
The Bravery of his faithful Mate
And at the same time Mark the Infamy of a
Savage Pirate
His afflicted Father ALEXANDER BARTLEMAN
Has ordered this stone to be erected over his
Honourable Grave

Wrecks And The Law

In the past, wrecks were regarded as a valuable resource by those living close to the sea. The laws surrounding them were complex and difficult to enforce. In 1477 the Pastons removed a lot of high quality timber which was washed up at Winterton from a wrecked cargo ship and local villagers 'stole' 22 cart loads. But, the local servant responsible said, 'I am threat to be troubled there, for there been 5 men alive on the ship.' In this letter to William Paston from Thomas, Earl of Surrey and later Duke of Norfolk, in the early sixteenth century, we see this issue raised. It is also interesting as a straightforward example of a great lord insisting on his feudal rights.

'Cousin Paston, I recommend me to you. And wheras as this summer there was a hulk of Humborowe perished before Winterton, and because that the men of the same was saved I might not claim the same as a wreck but commanded mine officers to restore the owners to their ship and goods belonging to the same, and since that time, as I am informed, Thomas Clere and Richard Palmer of Yarmouth bought the hull and masts with other tackle and timber belonging to the said ship; after which time with a raging tide part of the said ship was cast on land on your ground at Caister, which ye would withhold claiming the same to be your's as a wreck on your own ground.

Cousin Paston, I marvel ye do so, for as for wreck ye can prove it none, and if ye could it ought to be mine and not yours, for I am assured ye have no grant of the King nor of none of his antecessors kings of England to have wreck on your own ground ... Wherefore, cousin, I require you to restore the said Thomas and Richard unto their goods according to right ...'

A Great Fish

Whales are still occasionally stranded on the North Norfolk Coast but they are not now a valuable source of oil, so that we do not have unseemly arguments about the carcasses. This was not so in 1489, as this extract from a letter in the Paston papers demonstrates.

'... Sir, it is so that John Talyoure of Brytcham, deputy in your office of the Admiralty, was with me this morning to have mine advice in this matter following, the which is this.

There was taken against Thornham in the King's stream, lying 2 fathoms and a half deep upon the sea, a whale fish, by Thornham men labouring all night on Sunday night last was, and so have slain it and brought to lande; upon the which your deputy hath been there and seized my lord's part thereof . . . Then John a Lowe was there, and he said to your deputy that he would have the king's part in this wise, that the King and my Lord should part the half. Sir, the civil law sayeth thus: 'If any fish royal be found in the sea, that is to say whale, bales, sturgeon, porpoise or grampus, that my lord Admiral shall have the half part etc.' I think my lord hath the King's prerogative upon the sea . . .

It is a great fish and a royal. Your deputy showeth me it is 11 fathoms and more of length and 2 fathoms of bigness and deepness in the middle fish.'

An Accidental Death

In the 18th century the law could work surprisingly quickly and efficiently.

Sept 17, Friday

The young Woman Spincks (who lately had a Bastard Child by one Garthon of Norwich) called on me this morning to acquaint me that her Child is dead, died last night, supposed to her having given him a Sleeping Pill which she had of her Neighbour Nobbs whose Husband is very ill and had some composing Pills from Mr Thornes, one of which Nobbs wife advised her to give to her Child to put him to sleep whilst she was out. The Child slept for about 5 hours, then waked and fell into convulsion fits wch. continued for 4 Hours and half and then died in great Agonies. If the Child died owing to the effects of the Pill, I believe it not intentionally given to destroy the Child as she always had taken particular care of him and looked remarkably healthy. I advised her to make herself easy on that respect . . .

Sept 18, Saturday

. . . Mr Thorne called here about Noon having been to see the dead Child and said that its Death was owing to the Mothers giving it part of the Pill. Soon after the Doctor went, the Mother of the Child Eliz. Spincks came here to know what to do, I told her to go to the Overseer (Emery) to send for the Coroner and inspect the Body before I could bury it . . .

Sept 19, Sunday

... But few Farmers at Church this Afternoon on Account of an Inquest being taken by a Coroner from Norwich on the Body of Eliz. Spincks Boy. They were from 1. till near 5. on the above business. The Jury brought in their Verdict — not intentionally given by the Mother to her Child. This Evening between 6. and 7. I buried the Child (by name Garthon Spincks) in the Churchyard ...

(Parson Woodforde, 1790)

Some Memorable People

The Reeve

A Reeve was a sort of steward-cum-land agent for his lord. This one, from the Prologue to the Canterbury Tales, was, if hard-faced, obviously good at his job.

Hot-tempered was the Reeve and very thin,
No beard showed on his closely shaven chin.
Above his ears his hair abruptly stopped
And like a priest's his top was neatly cropped.
His legs were long and so extremely lean
They looked like sticks; no calf was to be seen.
His granaries and bins were kept with care;
No auditor could find an error there.
From observation of the drought and rain
He knew the likely yield of seed and grain.
His master's livestock, rams and ewes and cows
His bulls and bullocks, horses, chickens, sows
Were wholly under this Reeve's management.
He'd kept the books, under his covenant,
Since his young lord was in his twentieth year.
No man could ever catch him in arrear.
No baliff, herdsman, serf or dairymaid
Could fool him with the devious tricks they played.
Feared like the plague was he by common folk.
His lovely house sat on a heath where oak
And ash and maple shade the verdant pasture.
At business he was better than his master.
He had a pile locked in his private coffers.
And he could please his lord with subtle offers
Of helpful loans, and with this careful payment
He'd earn his thanks and even handsome raiment.
In youth he'd learned the useful trade and skill

Of carpentry, and he was expert still.
A horse called Scot bore this old Reeve along,
All dappled grey, a big and handsome stallion.
He wore a long surcoat of bluish shade,
And by his side he wore a rusty blade.
From Norfolk was this Reeve of which I tell:
He lived close by a town called Baldeswell.
He tucked up like a friar his coat of blue
And he was ever hindmost of our crew.

(Geoffrey Chaucer (c. 1340-1400))

Grandees

Sir Edward Coke (1552-1634) bought the Holkham estate in 1610: it has been in the same family's hands ever since. He was educated at Norwich Free School and at Cambridge. His first wife was Bridget Paston, who brought him considerable property. He held many important posts under Queen Elizabeth including Solicitor-General, Attorney-General and Speaker of the House of Commons. His law reports, which he began publishing in 1600, were instrumental in establishing the supremacy of Common Law in England. John Aubrey, in his Brief Lives, had some interesting things to say about him.

When I was first of the Middle Temple, I heard an old Lawyer, who was his country-man affirme that Sir Edward Coke, Knight, Lord Chief Justice of the King's Bench, was borne but to 300 pounds a yeare land, and I have heard some of his country say again that he was borne but to 40 pounds per annum. What shall one beleeve?

He left an estate of eleaven thousand pounds per annum, Sir John Danvers, who knew him, told me that he had heard one say to him, reflecting on his great scraping of wealth, that his sonnes would spend his Estate faster than he gott it; he replyed, They cannot take more delight in the spending of it than I did in the getting of it.

His second wife, Elizabeth, the relickt of Sir William Hatton, who was with Child when he maried her: laying his hand on her belly (when he came to bed) and finding a Childe to stirre, What, sayd he, Flesh in the Pott. Yea, quoth she, or els I would not have married a Cooke.

He shewed himself too clownish and bitter in his carriage to Sir Walter Ralegh at his Triall, where he sayes *Thou Traytor*, at every word, and *thou lyest like a Traytor*.

72

Sir Thomas Coke (1697-1759), created Earl of Leicester in 1744, was not entirely happy in the palace he had built at Holkham ...

It is a melancholy thing to stand alone in one's own country. I look around, not a house to be seen but my own. I am Giant of Giant Castle, and have ate up all my neighbours — my nearest neighbour is the King of Denmark.

A Hero's Funeral

Sir Christopher Myngs (1625-1666) came from Salthouse on the North Norfolk coast. He was made a vice-admiral in 1664 and received his death-wound in the Four Days Battle two years later. Extraordinarily, his flagship too was called the Victory. He was loved by his men, as Samuel Pepys noted in his diary on the 13th June.

After dinner ... to Sir Chr. Ming's Funerall, but find them gone to church. However I into church (which is a fair large church, and a great Chappell), and there heard the service and stayed till they buried him, and then out. And there met with Sir W. Coventry (who was there out of great generosity, and no person of quality there but he) and went with him into his Coach; and being in it with him, there happened this extraordinary case — one of the most Romantique that I ever heard of in my life, and could not have believed but that I did see it — which was this.

About a Dozen able, lusty, proper men came to the coachside with tears in their eyes, and one of them, that spoke for the rest, begun and says to Sir W. Coventry — "We are here a Dozen of us that have long known and loved and served our dead commander, Sir Chr. Mings, and have now done the last office of laying him in the ground. We would be glad we had any other to offer after him, and in revenge of him — all we have is our lives. If you will please to get his Royal Highness to give us a Fireshipp among us all, here is a Dozen of us, out of all which choose you one to be commander, and the rest of us, whoever he is, will serve him, and, if possible, do that that shall show our memory of our dead commander and our revenge." Sir W. Coventry was herewith much moved (as well as I, who could hardly abstain from weeping) and took their names; and so parted, telling me that he would move his Royal Highness as in a thing very extraordinary, and so we parted. The truth is, Sir Chr. Mings was a very stout man, and a man of great parts and most excellent tongue among ordinary men; and as Sir W. Coventry

says, could have been the most useful man in the world at such a pinch as this. He was come into great renowne here at home, and more abroad, as in the West Indys. He had brought his family into a way of being great. But dying at this time, his memory and his name (his father being always, and at this day, a Shoomaker, and his mother a Hoymans daughter, of which he was used frequently to boast) will be quite forgot in a few months, as if he had never been, nor any of his name be the better by it — he having not had time to collect any estate; but is dead poor rather than rich.

Note: A Hoyman was a man with a coaster, usually a sloop.

Sir Thomas At Home

In October 1671 John Evelyn travelled to Norwich, 'having a desire to see that famous Scholar and Physition Dr. T. Browne author of Religio Medici and Vulgar Errors etc: now lately knighted.'

Next morning I went to see Sir Tho. Browne (with whom I had sometime corresponded by Letters tho never saw before) whose whole house and Garden being a Paradise and Cabinet of rarities, and that of the best collection, especially Medails, books, Plants, natural things, did exceedingly refresh me after last nights confusion: Sir Thomas had amongst other curiosities, a collection of Eggs of all the foule and birds he could procure, that Country (especial the promontorys of Norfolck) being (as he said) frequented with severall kinds, which seldom or never, go farther into the Land, as Cranes, Storkes, Eagles etc: and variety of Water-foule: He likewise led me to see all the remarkeable places of this antient Citty, being one of the largest, and certainely (after London) one of the noblest of England, for its venerable Cathedrall, number of Stately Churches, Cleanesse of the streetes; and buildings of flint, so exquisitely headed and Squared, as I was much astonish'd at; Sir Tho. told me they had lost the art, of squaring the flint, which they once were so excellent in: and of which the Churches, best houses, and Walls are built: The Castle is an antique extent of ground, which now they call marsfield ... The suburbs are large, the prospect sweete, and other amoenities, not omiting the flower-gardens, which all the Inhabitans excell in of this Citty, the fabric of stuffs, which it affords the Merchants, and brings a vast trade to this populous Towne ... One thing I observ'd of remarkable in this Citty, that most of the Churchyards (though some of them large enough) were filled up with earth, or rather the congestion of dead body's one upon another, for want of Earth etc to the very top of the Walls, and many above the wales, so as the Churches seem'd to be built in pits.

A Rare Mind

Sir Thomas Browne (1605-1682) was a man of great wisdom as well as of great learning, a combination much rarer than most academics and literary critics suppose. His mind was generous and unprejudiced, which gives all the more force to his condemnation of mobs and contemporary Hooray Henries . . .

. . . I am of a constitution so general, that it consorts and sympathiseth with all things. I have no antipathy, or rather Idiosyncrasie, in dyet, humour, air, any thing. I wonder not at the French for their dishes of Frogs, Snails and Toadstools, nor at the Jews for Locusts and Grasshoppers; but being amongst them, make them my common Viands, and I find they agree with my stomach as well as theirs. I could digest a Salad gathered in a Church-yard, as well as in a Garden. I cannot start at the presence of a Serpent, Scorpion, Lizard, or Salamander: at the sight of a Toad or Viper, I find in me no desire to take up a stone to destroy them. I feel not in my self those common Antipathies that I can discover in others: those National repugnancies do not touch me, nor do I behold with prejudice the French, Italian, Spaniard, or Dutch: . . .

If there be any among those common objects of hatred I do contemn and laugh at, it is that great enemy of Reason, Virtue and Religion, the Multitude: that numerous piece of monstrosity, which, taken asunder, seem men, and the reasonable creatures of GOD; but, confused together, make but one great beast, and a monstrosity more prodigious than Hydra. It is no breach of Charity to call these *Fools*; it is the style all holy Writers have afforded them . . .

Neither in the name of *Multitude* do I onely include the base and minor sort of people; there is a rabble even amongst the Gentry, a sort of Plebeian heads, whose fancy moves with the same wheel as these; men in the same level with Mechanicks, though their fortunes do somewhat guild their infirmities, and their purses compound for their follies.

(Religio Medici)

The Norfolk Revolutionary

Tom Paine was born in Thetford in 1737 and died in New York State in 1809. His two best known books were Common Sense and The Rights of Man, both of which advocated republican government. Although considered a dangerous radical by the British authorities, most of his ideas are now the accepted common currency of politics in the West. He envisioned a property-owning democracy in which the worst inequalities of wealth would be reduced by progressive taxation. He believed that if all men had both a political and economic stake in society, they would naturally subordinate their personal interests to the good of the whole and that harmony would prevail. Although he is generally considered a hero of the left, his vision of society is surprisingly close to modern Toryism. In one area, however, his prophecies have not been fulfilled ...

Passing over, for the present, all the evils and mischiefs which monarchy has occasioned in the world, nothing can more effectually prove its uselessness in a state of civil government, than making it hereditary. Would we make any office hereditary that required wisdom and abilities to fill it? and where wisdom and abilities are not necessary, such an office, whatever it may be, is superfluous or insignificant.

Hereditary succession is a burlesque upon monarchy. It puts it in the most ridiculous light, by presenting it as an office which any child or idiot may fill. It requires some talents to be a common mechanic; but to be a king, requires only the animal figure of a man — a sort of breathing automaton. This sort of superstition may last a few years more, but it cannot long resist the awakened reason and interest of man.
(Rights of Man, Part Two. 1792)

A Polite Euphemism Leads To A Disappointment In Monochrome

The Miss Broomes lived in a Norfolk village where they ran a small, neat farm. Every Sunday they walked four miles to their Baptist chapel, clad alike in skirts of black silk ...

'Only once in the course of their existence has Hannah ever been known to speak on this long Sunday walk. There had been an unusual excitement among the chapel members, caused by an announcement that the annual missionary sermon would be preached by a 'coloured gentleman' — it was even placarded all over the village — and the little building was crammed to overflowing by an expectant congregation, very different from the usual slender company of the 'Chosen Few'. When the service was over, the sisters pushed out through the throng of loafers collected at the roadside to watch the departure of the Rev. Samuel Brogden (from Liberia), and plodded their homeward way in their habitual silence; but before it was time for the bag and umbrella to change places, Susan felt her shawl plucked from behind, and Hannah's voice broke the stillness.

"Seusan, didn't that say the preacher would be a coloured gentlemen?"

Susan nodded, and Hannah fell back for some minutes, and then again the hand in the black cotton glove was thrust upon Susan's arm, and this time there was a pathetic ring in Hannah's voice,

"Seusan, he warn't nuthin' but *black!*"

(Rev. A. M. Wilson. 1903)

The View From Outside

The Mysterious East

That Man of Parts, Alan Coren, took a look at East Anglia in All Except The Bastard (1976). A pedantic person might question the accuracy of his history, but there can be little doubt that he has the gift of prophecy.

What, exactly, is Orientalism? Is this word, coined by the West used to describe a *genuine* property, a queer, ancient compound exhaled by centuries of *moo goo gai pan* and paper flowers and atonal songs and ritual suicide? Something tangible which comes only with vertical language and exploding populations and paddy-fields and gnomic poetry? Or do we use the word to label, instead, some artificial quality imposed out of fear, ignorance and superciliousness by timid Occidentals on a rather simple agricultural civilisation about whose human fertility the West has recurrent saffron-coloured nightmares? After all, Christianity is far more complex and mysterious than Zen; Wittgenstein more labyrinthine than Confucius; Joyce more weird than Ts'ao Chan; and quails in aspic more abstruse than prawn chop suey. Whence, then, the mystery? Whence inscrutability?

Anyone maddened by the apparent irrelevance of such questions to the subject of Ipswich and Beccles should take a large map of the world and hold it up to a bright light. It will not be long before he is thunderbolted to the quick by the physical similarities between East Anglia and China. No other country in the world is shaped like these two huge eastern buttocks of land; and, if the sheer weight of geophysical evidence still hasn't convinced the sceptic of the analogy, let him examine the way in which the rest of England considers its Orient. It is virtually identical with the world's attitude to South-East Asia.

Both countries have suffered from the Western assumption that physical isolation automatically means temperamental isolation; the isolationism is, in fact, entirely Western in origin. And from this initial misrepresentation springs the familiar bifurcated attitude that what you do not understand must be either (a) mysteriously sinister or (b) hysterically funny. So into the joke-books of a billion Occidental Joe Millers goes the hilarious paraphernalia of, in the one case, yellow faces, sing-song voices, chop-sticks, rice-cultivation, pig-tails, comic peasants, and funny names (e.g. Hangchow, Nanking), and, in the other, red faces, rural burrs, clay pipes, turnip cultivation, tweed caps, comic farm-labourers, and funny names (e.g. Hockwold cum Wilton, Newton Flotman). As for the sinister aspect, this is also compounded of a thimbleful of half-digested facts, most of them topographical: East Anglia is seen as a great, flat soggy wilderness where bearded tits and bustards, not elsewhere found, croak and carol in the shrouding mists, where wild geese woo the moon, and where the sea laps hungrily at the reclaimed land it sees as its stolen property held at bay only by the actions of witches, warlocks and tiny hunchbacks with sprigs of mildewed bindweed.

The saddest feature of all this irresponsible myth-making is that the inhabitants of these countries ultimately begin to approximate to the myth image; if the outside world seeks to impose exclusiveness and oddity on you, then you may choose, out of bitterness, to manufacture your own brand of separatism. And, just as China, for so long mocked and rejected, has responded by widening the rift from its own side of the line, so, too, East Anglia has come to separate itself from Mother England. The process there, however, started much further back in time.

In 400,000 B.C., to judge from excavations at such thriving knapping-sites as Whitlingham, there was little to separate East Anglian Man from his siblings throughout the uncivilised world: a stooping, hirsute knotty character, with scant frontal projection and a limited vocabulary, he was slow to anger; to almost anything, in fact, except perhaps to the manufacture of flint axe-handles, with which the area is rife. He also perfected the Small Round Stone, used for braining anything that wandered past the front of his hole. He was, in short, no different from the run-of-the-mill prehistoric biped. However, one singularly important fact must not be overlooked: at this period, England was still joined to Scandinavia, and the bulk of the population inhabited its eastern side; but there were extensive squatter settlements dotted around the rest of prehistoric Britain. These Western people remained a rather aimless, negative race for several eons; they left very few axe-handles or even Small Round Stones and consequently cannot be considered anywhere near as sophisticated as the East Anglians. During the Mesolithic Period, between 10,000 and 50,000 B.C., the East Anglians were knocking up harpoons, hammers, tiny jugs, and rude sleds by the gross; and still nothing was going on in the West, except the production of throwing sticks, and a few square rocks probably used for smashing anything these small, moronic communities could lay their fumbling hands on.

By 10,000 B.C., however, Britain was beginning to separate from the mainland of Europe; the lowlands between started to fill up, first with salt marshes, later with lagoons, and finally, at one horrifying bound, the North Sea. This transitional period was a time of great stress for Meso-Neolithic East Anglian Man; some threw in their lot with the Continent, and, as the water rushed over their stricken lake-dwellings, they began splashing towards Denmark, Holland, and so on. Many, not quite trained to make even the simplest decisions, simply sat there while the stuff slopped up to their eyebrows, pondering the futility of Neolithic life, and quietly perished. The rest plumped for England. East Anglia was born; but now it was a minority area — suddenly, the cretinous, brutish oafs in the Western sector were top men on the totem. Prejudice was born. It was 9,086 B.C.

During the next few thousand years, the West was filled with a slowly evolving race of power-maniacs, elementary arms manufacturers, and, naturally, fighters. Woad-covered gangs of Bronze and Stone Age tearaways roamed the countryside hacking one another to pieces with crude swords, spears and choppers, and generally despising the mild men in the East who were preoccupied with stopping the sea from dining off their families, and with developing primitive agricultural systems and fishing boats. In the West, the pattern of the modern world was being created in all its bloody malevolence; in the East, man was meekly cultivating himself into obscurity. The Anglo-Saxon take-over in the East was a peaceful enough affair; and the subsequent pre-Norman punch-up between Mercians and Northumbrians and West Saxons left the East virtually unmarked. They accepted Christianity quietly, happily; it seemed, in all its fine impossible idealism, to be just what they were looking for; of the extant one hundred and eighty Saxon church-towers in England, one hundred and nineteen are in Norfolk alone. It might have been our Paradise; we lost it, and perhaps that lies behind much of our scornful separatism.

Gradually, during the Norman Period and the Early Middle Ages, the gulf widened. The Norman temperament was totally alien to the East Anglian; London, which by now had become the controlling centre of the country, paid no attention to East Anglia, except to blow the occasional Middle English raspberry towards the rural Orient. Little by little, the men of Suffolk and Norfolk let the iron corkscrew into their souls; the practical, optimistic ones decided to cut their cultural losses and conformed to the picture the West was forming of them: sullen men with knotty fingers and a predilection for simple, basic things. They went away, usually alone, to cross-breed pigs and cows and sheep; many succeeded, producing the Large Black pig, the Dun Cow, the Black-faced sheep, the Suffolk Punch horse; but many failed, and for years the country was infested with curious three-legged hybrids, miniature bulls, barking horses and hens that gave milk and went mad in the dark. Abortive animal husbandry created an even deeper sullenness and resentment in those sections of the population involved in the biological misery; it also gave rise to great waves of witchcraft, black and white, which, instead of clearing up the mess, worsened it. A village of some eight hundred souls in northern Norfolk became the disciples of a cow with two heads; when it died, the village broke up in disorder and its inhabitants scattered the madness in tiny dangerous fragments throughout East Anglia.

There was also, of course, serious revolt against the ridicule from the West. In 1549, Robert Kett raised 16,000 men outside Norwich in order to force the King's hand in giving a square deal to the peasants, whom the King, a lad of twelve, had no doubt only seen in primitive pantomimes and therefore considered to be an even bigger laugh than his elders did. After four thousand of the rebels were slaughtered, the rebellion folded. During the Civil War, Cromwell, a Huntingdon man whom many maleducated but socially eminent Londoners therefore thought of as a comic East Anglian, put Norfolk to the sword and the flame, merely in order to prove this particular point groundless. East Anglia has since been singularly unrebellious, restricting its open resentment to small pockets of resistance like that of William Dowsing, the Laxfield Puritan iconoclast who spent much of the seventeenth century in desecrating Suffolk churches for the glory of the Lord, George Crabbe, who employed the bulk of his poetry as a stick to beat Goldsmith's rural ignorance with, and the unknown madman who hung the bells in East Bergholt church upside down for reasons best known to himself, and then vanished.

East Anglia is, even more depressingly, an area deeply involved with death, dying and internment, a taste observable in so many Far Oriental societies for whom living is a wretched process the end of which is the only cause for celebration most of them ever have. The reason probably holds for Suffolk and Norfolk too. These counties are curiously proud of their ancient barrows, cairns and pits, which, seen close to, can be bitterly disappointing for the tourist, looking as they do either like unsuccessful bomb-shelters or like amateur elephant traps. Worse, from the beginning of the Great Social Rift, most of the East Anglian upper classes spent their time in commissioning horizontal statues of themselves to be placed on huge stone sarcophagi, in which they could be laid to rest, safe at last from the sarcasm of the West. The one great literary genius of Norfolk was Sir Thomas Browne, who made a career from the incessant contemplation of death (or Death, as they like to think of it locally); he at least came to terms with the gloominess of East Anglian life; but, inevitably, the oppressive mood comes through in such characteristically sour statements as 'Charity begins at home' (*Religio Medici)* 'For the world, I count it not an inn, but an hospital, and a place, not to live, but to die in' *(Ibid)* and 'Hercules is not only known by his foot'(*Urn Burial)*. And, despite his desire for translation to a better place than Norwich, he was nevertheless clearly disturbed at the possibility of 'that unextinguishable laugh in heaven' (*The Garden of Cyrus)*.

There really is no need to analyse what for want of a better word can be called modern East Anglia; everything is just as it was, a little gloomier, perhaps, a little more sullen, a little more fatalistic. The few optimists still pursue agricultural development, the ringing cadences of Turnip Townshend, Coke of Holkham and other sod-turning pioneers committed to faithful memory; the rest survive, and, each year, the really sour gather in small malicious groups on the Norfolk Broads to jeer at the aquatic inadequacy of the only West Anglians they ever get the chance to see.

It is not easy to predict how this slow, corrosive process will end; but it is just possible. Already East Anglia has put out a tentative feeler towards the twentieth century by building a fertiliser plant on advanced lines; but it has done this experimentally, half-heartedly. If the area is finally to be accepted as an unqualified (and, hence, uncomic, un-mysterious, and unalien) part of the country which for nigh on half a million years has looked on it as an embarrassment to England's dream of an industrial/militarist/progressive society, it must continue the con-forming process begun, so recently and so very late, with the construction of the nuclear-powered eyesore of Sizewell. It must build in the image west of its frontier. It must bulldoze unlandscaped concrete motor-ways across its churchyards and village greens; it must envelop its quiet country towns in openplan developments, tinfoil supermarkets, haphazard skyscrapers, bingoleums, bowling alleys, Hotscoff beefburger bars, drive-in laundromats, black concrete bus-garage; it must fill its unprofitable, wildfowl sanctuaries with billboards, neons, gas-stations, dog-tracks, industrial waste, jerry-built council estates, half-planned fac-tory areas, shoddy apartment-blocks, and death-heaps of rusting aban-doned cars.

It must, in short, Wake Up To The Facts Of Life Today And March Shoulder To Shoulder With The Rest Of Britain Into The Glorious Future.